WHERE SERFDOM THRIVES

The Plantation Tamils of Sri Lanka

Mayan Vije

Tamil Information Centre

Published by:-

Tamil Information Centre
Thulasi
Bridge End Close
Kingston Upon Thames
KT2 6PZ
www.ticonline.org

Editor :
S. Sivanayagam
Editorial Assistance :
A. Arulanandan
Design and Lay-out :
S. Anandamurugan
Typesetting
Art Prints, Madras.

November 1987

Here is no hamlet...
Nor deserted village
Where manhood grew...
Where history made
The sword and fire
Here is but a row
Of tin-roofed lines..
The very warehouse
Where serfdom thrives.
Within a scanty space
Of ten by twelve
There is the hearth home
Drenched in soot and smoke
To eat and sleep,
To incubate and breed
To meet master's greed
To meet master's greed

C.V. Velupillai
'IN CEYLON'S TEA GARDEN'

CONTENTS

TABLES

MAPS

PREFACE

The problems confronting the plantation Tamils are numerous and only a few are dealt with in this publication. Some of the aspects that are not included are given below :

Consequences of the Indo-Ceylon Agreement

Problems of repatriates

Working conditions

Problems arising from labour - management relations

Special problems of women and children

Consequences of the Land Reform Law and the establishment of various organisations such as the National Agricultural Diversification and Settlement Authority (NADSA)

The impact of national development schemes

Consequences of colonisation within estates

Consequences of divesting of estates under amendment to the Land Reform Law and fragmentation of estates

Impact of labour and other legislation

Further publications are planned on these issues depending on the availability of resources. The name 'Sri Lanka' is generally used in this publication and no distinction is made in this respect of the periods before and after the Republican Constitution of 1972 when the name of the country was changed from Ceylon to Sri Lanka.

The term 'plantation Tamils' is generally used, but in certain places in order to indicate the wider impact of the problems, the term 'persons of Indian origin' is employed. The terms 'plantation workers' is also used where the problem relates to employment.

The sufferings of the Sri Lankan Tamils have received world-wide attention while the tribulations of the plantation Tamils remain unexposed. This publication is an attempt to focus attention at least on some of the problems of the plantation Tamils.

September 1987   *Mayan Vije*

IX

1

SHORT HISTORY

The first coffee plantations in Sri Lanka were established in the 1820s, the first batch of South Indian Tamil labour arriving in 1823. The planters, during the colonial days found that it was impossible to recruit local Sinhalese labour. Several reasons are ascribed to the refusal of the Sinhala pesants to take up work on plantations. Ownership of cultivable land and the consequent absence of economic pressure is thought to be an important reason. The work on plantations necessitated the residing of the workers in barrack-like line rooms away from families for long periods. Strong family ties which required the presence of members of the family in social observance discouraged people from staying away from families.

The British colonialists had to look elsewhere for labour. Chinese labour was not preferred as the British were 'dissatisfied' with their work and due to the abolition of slavery in 1834 slaves from Africa could not be brought. The other alternative was South India and was preferred for its proximity.

Coffee reigned supreme from the 1820s and reached its peak in 1869 when 939,000 cwt was produced from 300,000 acres of coffee plantations. The following years saw the decline of coffee due to leaf fungus attack and by 1885 coffee was completely destroyed.

Planters looking for alternative crops chose tea and rubber. The districts of Kandy, Badulla and N'Eliya were found most suitable for tea plantations and Kegalle, Kalutara and Ratnapura districts for rubber plantations. In 1873, 280 acres were planted with tea and by 1915 it had increased to 426,000 acres and export of tea rose from 1,250,490 lbs in 1901 to 6,441,242 lbs in 1910. Rubber plantations increased from 705 acres in 1898 to 240,000 acres in 1915[1].

In order to facilitate large scale cultivation of this nature the colonial government enacted the Crown Lands (Encroachment) Ordinance in 1840, which made all forests, waste lands unoccupied or uncultivated lands as the property of the Crown. The lands acquired by the government under the Ordinance were sold to planters at 5 shillings an acre.[2] Waste lands Ordinance was enacted in 1897 which provided for acquisition by the Crown of undeveloped lands for which claims were not made within three months of a specified date.

These factors enormously enhanced the need to recruit more and more labour from South India, particularly the present Tamil Nadu. Planters adopted various methods to inveigle labour into Sri Lanka. The inherent poverty in the Madras Presidency at the time compounded by periodic droughts of a severe nature, the harsh Ryotwari Tax system, low wages, expanding population competing for scarce resources and the entrenched aspects of social structure such as the caste system simplified the task of recruitment.

Organised recruitment from South India began in 1837 and ended in 1939 when immigration of unskilled workers was banned. Although there was no legal sanction for emigration of workers to Sri Lanka in 1837 the Indian Government chose to ignore recruitment of workers. But as recruitment increased the Government was forced to intervene to enact Act XIII of 1847 which gave official sanction to emigration of labour to Sri Lanka. On the request of the Indian government the Sri

---

[1] 'Indians in Sri Lanka'   H P Chattopadhyaya, Page 15

[2] 'Sri Lanka: The National Question and the Tamil Liberation Struggle'   Satchi Ponnambalam, Page 7

Lankan government passed the Ordinance No. 3 of 1847 prohibiting workers to be sent beyond the shores to Sri Lanka.

The workers were mainly recruited in the districts of Chenkelpettai, Coimbatore, Madurai, North Arcot, Pudukottai, Ramanathapuram, Salem, South Arcot, Thanjavoor, Thirunelvely and Trichirapalli. A negligible number of workers were also recruited from the present states of Kerala, Karnataka and Andhra Pradesh. The main recruiting ground was the districts around Trichy which supplied 75% of the labour.

Recruitment of labour from South India was done by the Kangany System (Kangany in Tamil means an overseer or supervisor). A Kangany was sent by the planter to South India to recruit labour. In earlier times the Kangany recruited his kinsmen and persons from nearby villages. Because of this it was not uncommon to find most workers on an estate being related to each other. Later as the need for labour increased and with the establishment of the Ceylon Labour Commision, Kanganies began to recruit even outside their clans and villages. The Ceylon Labour Commission was established in 1904 under the Coast Agency Committee of the Planters' Association, which functioned from Trichy and supervised recruitment of labour. After 1904 the Kangany had to in the first instance obtain a licence from the Controller of Indian Immigrant Labour in Sri Lanka. The lincence if in order was then endorsed by the Ceylon Labour Commission. The Kangany after recruitment had to obtain the approval of the village Munsiff and bring the recruits before the Labour Commission for inspection[3].

Before the introduction of this procedure the Kangany recruited any one he wished and there was no proper check. Even the introduction of the procedure did not prevent the exploitation of the workers by the Kangany. The Kangany paid

[3] Chattopadhyaya, op.cit., **Page 44**

an advance to the worker at the time of recruitment. This advance, the cost of journey, half of the cost of food supplied and any other expenses relating to recruitment were all debited to the worker's account on the estate. Therefore the worker on arrival on the estate began life in debt.

A system called Tin-ticket system was introduced in 1902 in order to prevent any delays of the recruits arriving in Sri Lanka. Under this system the Sri Lankan government took responsibility of transporting the recruits to Sri Lanka and recovered the cost later from superintendents. The worker was issued a 'tin ticket' which he had to present at the quarantine camp at Mandapam or Tataparai. Thereafter he was given food and transported to Sri Lankan shores and then to the estate. This system has been compared to the value-payable by post (VPP) system, the worker being delivered like a parcel[4].

The workers travelled from their villages to Mandapam or Tataparai quarantine camp (later only Mandapam camp was used to quarantine workers) and quarantined for six days. Then they were taken by ferry across to Talaimannar along the Pampan-Dhanushkodi route. From Talaimannar the recruits walked all the way to Kandy, more than 150 miles away, through thick jungles infested with wild animals. (see Grandmother's story in 'Whose Paradise' by Stella Hillier and Lynn Gerlach-Minority Rights Group, London 1987). From Kandy the workers were sent to various estates. H.P. Chattopadhyaya writes about the journey of the workers:

"A considerable part of the long route lay through comparatively unhealthy and desolate districts without practically any shelter to be found on the wayside, and without water for miles ahead. The journey through such inhospitable districts caused the labourers untold sufferings which were aggravated

---

4 ibid., Page 47

by their extreme poverty, with the result that many died of exhaustion and cholera on the way, their mortal remains not infrequently lying unburied on the road-side. Those who reached their destination felt so much run down and became so much emaciated by disease and starvation that they were quite unable to work on estates for some days and consequently faced privation and hardship".[5]

On arrival the workers had to live in barrck-like line rooms and had to face the cold climate. Their exploitation continued in several ways. One of them was the tundu (chit) system. The tundu system was a method by which the indebtedness of the worker was perpetrated. Gnanamuttu describes the tundu system:

"With the institution of the head kangany system came the pernicious tundu system based on the labourer's indebtedness to the kangany, from whom he would have initially borrowed money in order to settle his debts in the village before he could leave it, and to pay the cost of his outward journey. To these debts would be added sundry borrowings for weddings, funerals, coming-of-age ceremonies and the cost of goods bought in the estate kadai (or shop) owned by the kangany. A planter who required the services of a gang of labourers would pay the kangany the total amount the gang owed him; he would then assume the role of creditor, and proceed to recover from his labourers the moneys they would now owe him. No new employer would take these workers into his service without a tundu or chit from their employer to the effect that he was prepared to release them on being paid the amount that was owing to him (as stated in the tundu). In times of labour shortage it was not unusual for planters to seek the services of a gang of labourers by offering to pay the kangany sums in excess of the total amount that was due to him from his labourers, and for the kangany to go about trying to sell the

---

services of himself and of his gang to the highest bidder".[6]

Although the tundu system was abolished in 1921, there was no ending to the indebtedness of the worker.

The sufferings of the plantation Tamil worker was made worse by low wages and appalling living conditions (which persist to this day) and there was no organised representative body to represent matters on their behalf. The vacuum was filled in July 1939 by the formation of the Ceylon Indian Congress (CIC) and the Ceylon Indian Congress Labour Union in March 1940, the former a ,political party and the latter its trade union wing and large number of plantation workers joined these organisations.

In 1950 the Ceylon Indian Congress was renamed as Ceylon Workers Congress and due to internal squabbles the union split in 1956 leading to the formation of the Democratic Workers Congress (DWC). The CWC split once again and another trade union the National Union of Workers (NUW) was formed. After some plantation workers obtained Sri Lankan citizenship it became necessary for political parties to woo them and each political party formed its own trade union in the plantations including the two major parties the Sri Lanka Freedom Party (SLFP) and the United National Party (UNP). Today there are, in the plantations as many as twenty five trade unions. It is not uncommon to find several trade unions on one estate, giving an opportunity for the superintendent of the estate to play one against the other to jeopardise the interest of the workers. At the same time, as it often occurs, on common issues trade unions at local level together formulate common strategies to win their demands. The rivalry at national level is much fiercer sometimes resulting in complete disregard of the interest of the workers. Two instances may be quoted in

[6] 'Education and Indian Plantation worker in Sri Lanka' - G A Gnanamuttu, Page 5

this regard. In 1974 the CWC organised a strike on several demands, chief among them being reasonable working hours and monthly wages. After the strike continued for several days, the DWC decided to join the strike. But immediately the CWC withdrew from the strike without any of the major demands being met. In 1986 the CWC gave notice of strike demanding higher wages. This measure was supported by another major union in the plantations, the Lanka Jathika Estate Workers Union (LJEWU). But two days before the commencement of the strike the LJEWU accepted the offer of the employers for a nominal increase in the wages and withdrew from the strike without consultation with the other unions. (See chapter on wages). Although trade unions have brought about improvement in wages, conditions of employment and other aspects, fragmentation of the trade unions and the rivalry between them have been major obstacles in winning important rights for the workers.

In 1948 and 1949 the plantation Tamils were rendered stateless and voteless by legislation and in 1964 and 1974 they were the subjects of two agreements between the governments. of India and Sri Lanka. These matters and some of the important problems affecting the plantation Tamils are dealt with in the following chapters.

2

CITIZENSHIP

The single act of discrimination which reduced the plantation workers and other people of Indian origin to mere slaves and devastated their lives was the enactment of the Citizenship Act in 1948.

Following the resolution of the Imperial Conference held in 1921 in London, which reaffirmed the resolution of the Imperial War Conference of 1918, Sri Lanka was agreeable to grant citizenship to the plantation Tamil population. During that period, to exercise the right to vote, an elector should have the following qualifications:

1. Ability to read and write English, Sinhala or Tamil and

2.a) Annual income of Rs.600 or
   b) Ownership of immovable property to the value of Rs.1500/- after allowing for any mortgage debts, or
   c) Occupation as owner or tenant for six months before the preparation of the electoral register, of a house of annual value of Rs.400/- if situated within the limits of the Municipality or local board or Rs.200/- if situated elsewhere.

The plantation workers did not possess any of these qualifications and were not eligible to vote in general elections. Although they did not qualify to vote they had all the other rights of a British subject.

In 1931 'Universal adult franchise' was granted in Sri Lanka and the Royal Commission for Constitutional Reform (Donoughmore Commission-appointed in 1928) recommended that voting right be granted on the basis of residence of five or more years (with temporary absence for 8 months throughout the 5 years), and confine such right to those who had an abiding interest in the country or who may be regarded as permanently settled in the Island and proposed that the property and literacy qualifications be dropped.

The recommendations of the Donoughmore Commission were severely contested by the Sinhalese members of the legislative council when debated in 1929 on the ground that such measures would virtually grant citizenship to all persons of Indian origin and consequently affect the votes of the Kandyan Sinhalese. The Legislative Council after debating the issue imposed the following conditions:

1) Minimum age of qualification for franchise should be 21 for both male and female.

2) Every voter should be able to read and write English, Sinhalese or Tamil.

On further demand of the Sinhalese people and on the recommendation of the Governor Sir Herbert Stanley the then government imposed two alternative requirements in 1930 for undomiciled persons:

1) Literacy and property qualifications or

2) Certificate of permanent settlement certifying

   a) five years residence.

   b) declaration of intention to permanently reside in the island.

   c) renunciation of claim of protection of any government other than Sri Lanka.

(Sections 4,5,6 & 7 of the Ceylon (Parliamentary Elections) Order in Council 1946).

These conditions in effect eroded the franchise rights of the plantation Tamils. Moreover, the taking of the certificate of permanent settlement would have been regarded as confirming an undomiciled status. In this context it may be pointed out that three commissions had concluded that a substantial number of people of Indian origin were permanently resident in Sri Lanka contrary to the clamour of Sinhalese politicians that their loyalty lay elsewhere:

1) The Royal Commission on Constitutional Reform (Donoughmore Commission) in its report published in July 1928 estimated that 40-50% of the people of Indian origin were permanent residents of Sri Lanka.

2) The report of the Commission on Immigration into Ceylon (Jackson Report) published in 1938 stated that 60% of the people of Indian origin were permanently settled (Ceylon Sessional Paper 111 - 1938).

3) The Report of the Soulbury Commission (1944-45) reported that 80% were permanently resident.

Therefore most plantation Tamils preferred to register as voters on the strength of domicile. As the number of plantation Tamil voters increased opposition to registration intensified and various restrictions were placed for registration which consequently reduced the number of plantation Tamil voters. Attempts were also made to repatriate some of the workers and to deny them franchise at local government level. The latter attempt proved successful. Europeans, Burghers and the plantation Tamils could not participate in any local government committees in terms of Village Committees Ordinance of 1889. This Ordinance was amended in 1937 and franchise at village level was granted to Europeans and Burghers, but the Tamil plantation workers were excluded. Later, due to continued protests the Ordinance was further amended to exclude all plantation workers voting in local elections. As there were only a few Sinhalese workers on plantations, this measure affected mainly the Tamil workers. The plantation Tamils including those who had obtained Sri Lankan Citizenship remained voteless at local government elections until 1981 when an amendment to the Local Government Elections Act granted voting rights at local elections to plantation Tamils who had obtained citizenship of Sri Lanka.

In 1931, 100,000 persons of Indian origin had been registered as voters and voted at the Legislative Council elections in that year. Representing these people, S.P. Vythilingam (Talawakelle) and M. Peri Sundaram (Hatton) were elected and the latter was appointed Minister of Labour, Industry and Commerce in the State Council. The number of voters of Indian origin in 1936 had risen to 145,000 and in the elections during that year again two persons to represent the people of Indian origin were elected. They were S.P. Vythilingam (Talawakelle) and K. Natesa Aiyar (Hatton).

In the 1947 general elections the Ceylon Indian Congress (CIC) which has been formed in 1939 as a political organisation to represent the plantation workers contested and won seven seats in Parliament. The seven members of Parliament were S. Thondaman (Nuwara Eliya), C.V. Velupillai (Talawakelle), K. Kumaravelu (Kotagala), K. Rajalingam (Nawalapitiya), G.R. Motha (Maskeliya), D. Ramanujam (Aluthnuwara) and S.M. Subbiah (Badulla). After the deprivation of citizenship in 1948 and disenfranchisement of the plantation Tamils in 1949, not until 1977 was a person directly elected to Parliament by the Plantation Tamils (S. Thondaman N'Eliya/Maskeliya), although members have been nominated to parliament to represent the plantation Tamils during the intervening years.

The Citizenship Act which came into operation on 21st September 1948 created two categories of citizenship - the acquisition of citizenship by descent and registration. In the case of citizenship by descent, the law specified 15 November 1948 as the appointed date and distinguished those born in the country from those born outside the country, thus creating four ways of acquisition of citizenship by descent:

1) A PERSON BORN IN SRI LANKA BEFORE 15TH NOVEMBER 1948

Such person was a citizen by descent if

a) his father was born in Sri lanka or

b) his paternal grandfather and paternal great-grandfather were born in Sri Lanka. Section 4 (1)

2) A PERSON BORN OUTSIDE SRI LANKA BEFORE 15TH NOVEMBER 1948

Such person was a citizen by descent if

a) his father and paternal grandfather were born in Sri Lanka or

b) his paternal grandfather and paternal great-grandfather were born in Sri Lanka. Section 4 (2)

3) A PERSON BORN IN SRI LANKA ON OR AFTER 15TH NOVEMBER 1948

* Such person was a citizen by descent if at the time of his birth his father was a citizen of Sri Lanka. Section 5

4) A PERSON BORN OUTSIDE SRI LANKA ON OR AFTER 15TH NOVEMBER 1948

* Such person was a citizen by descent if at the time of his birth his father was a citizen of Sri Lanka. Section 5

(* For these categories birth must be registered within one year at the office of the consular officer of Sri Lanka in the country of birth or at the office of the Minister in Sri Lanka - Section 5 (2))

A person may apply to become a citizen by registration under the Act if

a) he is of full age and sound mind and

either

b) his mother is or was a citizen by descent or would have been if she had been alive on the appointed date, and

c) he, being married, has been resident in Ceylon throughout the immediately preceding seven years or being unmarried has been so resident for a period of 10 years

or

d) he is the spouse or a widow or widower of a citizen, and

e) he has been resident in Ceylon throughout the immediately preceding one year

or

f) he is a person who ceased to be a citizen by descent upon acquiring citizenship of another country and has thereafter renounced that citizenship (repealed by amendment Act No.10 of 1950)

or

g) he is a person who has rendered distinguished public service or is eminent in professional, commercial, industrial or agricultural life but is otherwise ineligible to apply for citizenship by registration.

and

h) he is and intends to continue to be, ordinarily resident in Sri Lanka.

The provisions of the Citizenship Act as seen above are extremely rigid and it was almost impossible to obtain citizenship under both categories. Under the law there was no possibility of obtaining citizenship on the basis of a person's birth in Sri Lanka. Registration of births began only after 1895 with the enactment of the Registration of Births Ordinance and therefore it was impossible to prove births of the paternal grandfather and paternal great grandfather. Majority of the workers did not have their birth certificates or their fathers' birth certificates. Although the Citizenship Act, being an enactment of the Parliament, applied to all persons in Sri Lanka, only the Tamils of Indian origin were called upon to prove their citizenship. It is to be noted that if all persons in Sri Lanka were required to prove their citizenship many of the Sinhalese people would not have been able to do so.

There were also other differences between the two categories of citizenship apart from the mode of acquisition, in that citizenship by registration was lesser of the two insofar as security was concerned. A person who has obtained citizenship by registration and renounces it could not resume citizenship whereas a citizen by descent could do so. If a citizen by registration resides outside Sri Lanka for five consecutive years he loses his citizenship. Furthermore the Minister has the power under the Act to end the citizenship by registration under certain circumstances (sections 8, 23 and 24). Under Section 8 (1) he could reject the application without assigning any reason for such rejection.

The Citizenship Act did not provide for acquisition of citizenship by birth and excluded the concept of commonwealth citizenship. There is no doubt that the Act was enacted in order to exclude most of the people of Indian origin, despite their birth and/or long period of residence in the island and the fact that they knew no/other home than Sri Lanka. This is confirmed by the statement of L.L.T. Peiris, the former Assistant Secretary of the Citizenship Division:

"The restrictive nature of the Ceylon law is attributable to the fact that, at the time the Act was passed, nearly one million persons living in Ceylon, out of the total population of approximatley ten million, were persons who had immigrated to Ceylon in recent times and their absorption would have adversely affected the interests of the indigenous population. It was apparently for this reason that no provision was made for the acquisition of citizenship by birth and acquisition by descent was restricted to persons who could show their ties with the country for at least two generations".[7]

In the beginning of 1949 the government having successfully "stemmed the swamping" by the plantation Tamils and following discussions with the Indian government, proceeded to enact another citizenship law, the Indian and Pakistani (Citizenship) Act No.3 of 1949 which came into force on 15 August 1949. This Act provided for acquisition of citizenship by registration:

1) The applicant should be of Indian or Pakistani origin and settled permanently in Sri Lanka.

2)a) If he is married he should have uninterrupted residence in Ceylon without continuous absence for a period of 12 months (section 3 (3)) for seven years prior to 1st January 1948 (Section 3 (1))

b) If unmarried he should have uninterrupted residence for ten years prior to 1st January 1948 (Section 3 (2))

3) If the applicant is a married male, his wife and minor children, if any, should also have been ordinarily resident in Sri Lanka.

4) Applicant must have an assured income of a reasonable amount or suitable business or employment, or other lawful means of livelihood, and

5) The application should have been made between 15 August 1949 and 14 August 1951.

6) The applicant should be free from any incapacity or disability which might render it difficult or impossible for him to live in Sri Lanka.

---

[7] 'The Citizenship Law of the Republic of Sri Lanka' L L T Peiris, Page 6

7) Provision was also made for appeal to the Supreme Court within three months of the decision of the Commissioner, for the Registration of Persons of Indian and Pakistan Residents.

These stringent provisions made it extremely difficult to obtain citizenship under the law. This was compounded by the decision of the Ceylon Indian Congress (CIC) which was the representative organisation of the plantation Tamils at that time. The CIC decided to ignore the call for applications under the Act and instructed its members not to make applications. A week before the deadline (the deadline was 14 August 1951) the CIC reversed its decision and called its membership to send in the applications. There was a frantic rush. CIC officials visited each area and collected applications to be handed over to the Department. This action itself might have caused the loss of many applications as they were not sent by registered post. When the final count was taken 237,034 applications had been made requesting citizenship for 825,000 (90%) persons of Indian origin.

Despite the enthusiastic response by the plantation Tamils which clearly showed their intention to continue to reside in Sri Lanka, the vast majority of the applications were rejected on flimsy grounds. Many were unable to produce evidence of their births in the island. A large number of applications were rejected on the ground that the applicants failed to establish that they were resident uninterruptedly for the prescribed period or to provide proof that they had an assured income of a reasonable amount. Technicality of the law was used to reject many applications. Chattopadhyaya refers to instances where applications were rejected for the alleged reason that signatures of the Justices of the Peace were not legible. The majority of the applicants whose applications had been rejected were plantation workers and they did not have the financial means to appeal against the decision of the Commissioner to the Supreme Court.

In November 1949 the government of Sri Lanka dealt the third blow on the plantation Tamils by the enactment of the Parliamentary Elections (Amendment) Act No.48 of 1949. The Ceylon Parliamentary Elections Order in Council of 1946 had provided that every British subject resident in Sri Lanka for six months, or otherwise qualified will have the right to vote at elections and also to hold political office. The Parliamentary Elections (Amendment) Act amended the Order-in-Council to provide that a person should be a citizen of Sri Lanka in order to have his name entered in the electoral register (Section 4 (1)). In the case of Duraiswamy vs Commissioner for the Registration of Indian and Pakistani Residents (1955   56 NLR 313), it was noted by Gratien J. that the amendment Act had the "effect of disenfranchising many Indian Tamils (and indirectly their descendants) in spite of their long residence in Ceylon". In another case Mudanayake vs Sivagnanasunderam (1951 - 53 NLR 25), it was argued on behalf of a Tamil of Indian origin named Kodakkan Pillai that the Citizenship Act and the Parliamentary Elections (Amendment) Act were both repugnant to section 29 of the Soulbury Constitution which prohibited the enactment of any law having the effect of removing or conferring any privilege or advantage on a particular community. The Supreme Court in rejecting these arguments stated that the facts which qualify or disqualify a person to be a citizen or voter have no relation to a community as such but they relate to his place of birth and to the place of birth of his father, grandfather or great grandfather which would equally apply to persons of any community. On appeal the Privy Council held that the migratory habits of the Indian Tamils are facts which are directly relevant to the question of their suitability as citizens of Ceylon and have nothing to do with them as a community". (Kodakkan Pillai vs Sivagnanasunderam 1953 - 54 NLR 433).

As stated earlier there is overwhelming evidence that the citizenship and the franchise Acts were designed to affect only the Tamils of Indian origin and the view of the Supreme

Court that it applied to everyone in the island is untenable. The Tamils of Indian origin had been long regarded as a separate community with special problems and as pointed out earlier three commissions had decided that a substantial number of members of that community were resident permanently in Sri Lanka. The Privy Council failed to consider these points and meted out gross injustice to the plantation Tamils. Referring to the Citizenship issue Nihal Jayawickrama states as follows:-

"It would appear that both courts (the Supreme Court and the Privy Council) were unduly influenced by the fact that the impugned legislation related to citizenship of a newly independent country. But it is precisely in respect of such vital matters that a community requires to be protected against discriminatory treatment. On this occasion, both courts failed to accord that protection and thereby rendered nearly a million people stateless."

The Immigrants and Emigrants (Amendment) Act No.16 of 1955 was another of the series of legislative measures directed against the Tamils of Indian Origin. The Immigrants and Emigrants Act. No.20 of 1948 which came into force on 1st November 1949 prohibited non-citizens from entering Sri Lanka without a passport and a visa or residence permit. Section 14 (3) (b) of this Act provided that 'no temporary residence permit shall be refused in the case of a person who, being a British subject was ordinarily resident in Ceylon for a period of at least five years immediately preceding the appointed date'.

The amending Act of 1955 substituted a new section for Section 14 and the new section provided for visas for persons entering Sri Lanka and did not have any provision similar to section 14 (3) (b). This amending Act in effect took away the right of Tamils of Indian origin who were resident in the island for more than five years, to continue to stay on temporary residence permit. Several of the applications for extension of residence permits were refused and consequently the validity of the amending Act was challenged in Courts in the case of

Meera *vs* Dias (1957 58 NLR 571) on the ground that it conferred on other communities a privilege which was denied to the members of the Indian community, thus contravening section 29 of the Soulbury Constitution. Once again the Supreme Court denied justice to an entire community confirming fears that it was becoming part and parcel of a system designed to discriminate against the Tamils of Indian origin. The Court held that the discrimination was between citizens and non-citizens and the legislature was free to confer rights or privileges exclusively on citizens or to impose restrictions or disabilities applicable solely to non-citizens. The Supreme Court failed to take into account the facts that section 14 (3) (b) of the 1948 Act mainly benefitted members of the community of Tamils of Indian origin who could not obtain citizenship under the rigorous provisions of the Citizenship Act of 1948 and that the other communities were not affected by the amending Act.

The problems created by legislation removing citizenship and disenfranchisement were enormous and the plantation Tamil community which was undergoing immense suffering by several handicaps heaped on them, sunk to a new depth of agony. These legislative measures caused hardship even to persons of Indian origin who had obtained citizenship. They are always called upon to produce their certificate of citizenship without which they could not undertake business, profession, education etc. This position of the persons who had become citizens of Sri Lanka worsened when the Supreme Court once again become party to the perpetration of discrimination. In Pasangna *vs* Registrar-General (1965 - 67 NLR 33) the Supreme Court of Sri Lanka held that the son of an Indian Tamil registered as a citizen of Sri Lanka under the Indian and Pakistani Residents (Citizenship) Act, must be described in the birth register maintained under the Births and Deaths Registration Act as the son of 'Indian Tamils'. Although the Supreme Court said in this case that the decision would not cause prejudice to such a person as citizens, in practice this has been used by state officers to resort to discrimination against the Tamils of

Indian origin.

Some of the problems of the stateless persons are listed below:

a) PURCHASE OF PROPERTY

When purchasing property a person of Indian origin has to submit his birth certificate and the certificate of citizenship to the Notary Public who would certify on the deed and note the number of the certificate. If he was stateless then he was required to pay a 100% tax on the value of the property, in terms of the provisions of the Finance Act of 1967 which were applicable to foreigners. Most of the Plantation Tamils were not affected by this provision as they were too poor to purchase any property at all.

b) ADOPTION OF CHILDREN

For Sri Lanka citizens proceedings for adoption of children may be commenced before any District Court; but foreigners could bring adoption action only before the District Court of Colombo. This provision which applies to foreigners applies in the case of stateless persons. A stateless person wishing to adopt a child has to travel to Colombo and begin proceedings there at great cost.

c) FOREIGN TRAVEL

Stateless persons could not obtain travel documents and consequently could not travel outside. Hundreds of thousands of people were confined to the island since 1948 upto 1978. After the promulgation of the 1978 constitution, those stateless persons who had applied for Sri Lanka citizenship under the Indo-Ceylon Agreement of 1964 (Sirimavo-Shastri Pact) were allowed to obtain an identity certificate (not a passport) which could be used to make only one journey to a foreign country. Those who had applied for Indian citizenship, those who did not apply for either country and those whose applications had been rejected remain confined to the island. The identity certificates issued are not recognised as authentic travel documents by several countries (eg. Singapore) and there have been instances where stateless persons have not been allowed to enter the foreign country, held at the airports and returned to Sri Lanka.

d) EDUCATION

In Sri Lanka free education up to the university level is provided to Sri Lankan citizens and stateless persons are not entitled to free education at university level. A fee is levied by the universities from stateless persons whose financial position is far inferior to the other entrants.

Stateless students are also not entitled to scholarships provided by the government and cannot obtain Bank loans like other students for the purpose of education, because Banks regard them as unlikely to obtain employment during the course of which the loan could be repaid.

e) EMPLOYMENT

Stateless persons are not entitled to employment in the state sector and the opportunities in the private sector are also extremely low as a result of private sector institutions conforming to government policy.

Stateless persons cannot obtain employment abroad because of the problem in obtaining travel documents.

f) TRADING

Stateless persons are not entitled to carry on export and import trade because licences are not issued to them.

h) GRANT OF STATE LANDS

Stateless persons are not entitled to land grants from the state.

i) FRANCHISE

After the denial of franchise rights to the plantation Tamils the number of seats in parliament representing Tamils was drastically reduced and the benefit accrued to the Sinhalese. After the 1947 general elections the Tamils (plantation Tamils and the Sri Lankan Tamils) had 20 seats in parliament but after the 1952 elections they were reduced to 13, whereas the seats for the Sir halese increased from 68 in 1947 to 75 in 1952. After the 1977 elections the Sinhalese with 72% of the population held 80% of the seats while Tamils with 20% of the population held only 12% of the seats (Even these Tamils lost their seats after the sixth Amendment to the Constitution in 1983) (See Table XIV in the Appendix). Without parliamentary and local government representation it is impossible for the community to obtain any benefits, take part in national development projects and to debate issues affecting the community in parliament and outside.

The demonstrations carried out by the Tamil leaders in protest against the citizenship and franchise Acts appear to be insignificant in comparison to the magnitude of the injustice caused to the plantation Tamils. The Ceylon Indian Congress launched a Satyagraha movement as late as in 1952 (29 April 1952). Members of the Congress assembled in front of the Parliament and the Prime Minister's office and they were dispersed by the police. On 16 September 1952 the congress suspended the Satyagraha campaign after assurance of the then Prime Minister Dudley Senanayake that applications for Sri Lankan citizenship would be expedited. Thereafter there was no mass protest against the denial of citizenship by any trade union or political organisation until 1986.

The indigenous Tamils who were in a more influential position did not give sufficient support to the plantation Tamils either. Some Sri Lankan Tamils parliamentarians in fact voted in favour of the discriminatory legislation. Kumari Jayawardene writes about the voting of these Tamil leaders:

"On the first Citizenship Act in August 1948, the two Tamil Ministers in the UNP government, C.Suntharalingam and C.Sittampalam voted 'aye' but refrained from speaking in the debate. While the Tamil Congress, led by G.G.Ponnambalam, voted against, C. Suntharalingam, who had serious reservations about the question, resigned from the government and G.G. Ponnambalam was made a Minister soon after. When it came to voting on the Indian Residents Act in December 1948, Ponnambalam voted for the bill, while S.J.V. Chelvanayakam of the Tamil Congress continued to vote against".[8]

Different views in this regard resulted in the split of the Tamil Congress. S.J.V. Chelvanayakam left the Tamil Congress in 1949 and formed the Federal Party.

Several discussions regarding the plantation Tamils between the Sri Lankan and Indian governments were held in the years that followed. Dudley Senanayake had discussions with C.C Desai, the Indian High Commissioner in April 1953 which was resumed at a meeting of Dudley Senanayake and Jawaharlal Nehru in London in June 1953, but there was no outcome in these talks.

In January 1954 Nehru had discussions in New Delhi with the new Prime Minister of Sri Lanka, Sir John Kotelawala and the discussions ended in the Indo-Ceylon Agreement of 1954 (Nehru-Kotelawala Pact). Important Provisions of the agreement are:

a) Both governments will check and suppress illicit immigration between the two countries.

b) Every endeavour will be made for the registration of citizens

---

8 'Ethnic and Class Conflicts in Sri Lanka   Kumari Jayawardena', Page 55

under the Indian and Pakistani Residents (Citizenship) Act, within two years.

c) Those persons who are not registered as citizens of Ceylon, may register themselves with the Indian High Commissioner as citizens of India.

d) Those registered as citizens of Ceylon will be placed in separate electoral register. Only if their number does not exceed 250, in any electorate, they would be placed in the national electoral register.

This agreement was not the final solution to the problem of the people of Indian origin. Between 1951 and 1962 only 132,312 persons had been granted Sri Lankan citizenship and only 35,411 had been recognised as Indian citizens under the Indian and Pakistani Residents (Citizenship) Act. This left the vast majority of the people of Indian origin to suffer the stigma of statelessness. In 1964 the Indian and Sri Lankan governments estimated that there were 975,000 stateless persons in Sri Lanka and in October 1964 (30.10.64) Prime Ministers of India and Sri Lanka entered into an agreement regarding the estimated 975,000 stateless persons. The salient features of Indo-Ceylon Agreement of 1964 (Sirimavo-Shastri Pact) are as follows :-

a) 300,000 persons and their natural increase would be granted Sri Lanka citizenship.

b) 525,000 persons and their natural increase would be accepted as citizens of India.

c) The status of the balance of 150,000 would be decided later.

d) Repatriation of those who are granted Indian citizenship would be phased over a period of 15 years.

e) Those to be repatriated would be granted free visa, same facilities enjoyed by the citizens of Sri Lanka and normal facilities of residence by the government of Sri Lanka, until they are repatriated. They would also be continued in their employment until repatriation.

f) Repatriates would be allowed to repatriate their assets including gratuity and provident fund and the maximum amount to be repatriated would not be less than 400 rupees per family.

The Sirimavo-Shastri agreement was concluded without any consultation with the people involved (ie. the plantation Tamils) or their representatives. Even the president of the Ceylon Workers Congress, S. Thondaman, who was an appointed member of parliament was not invited to participate in the negotiations and the people were divided between the two countries like chattel. The United Front for Repatriate Workers referring to the agreements of 1964 and 1974 in its Report of Activities (31-12-86) states thus : "It is evident from these agreements that the two nations have been paying particular attention in dividing the number of persons between themselves without displaying concern whatsoever to the plight of the people involved." Although the trade unions complained bitterly about non-consultation, there was no appreciable protest from them for this injustice. The Sri Lankan Tamil leaders for their part were satisfied by merely issuing statements.

The Indo-Ceylon Agreement (Implementation) Act No. 14 of 1967 (came into force on 5.6.1967) while giving legal recognition to the Indo-Ceylon Agreement of 1964 provided that four persons would be granted Sri Lanka citizenship for every seven persons admitted to Indian citizenship although the Agreement had envisaged the granting of Sri Lanka citizenship in proportion to the actual number of persons repatriated to India. Therefore in this respect the Act differed from the Agreement and from the point of view of the plantation Tamils was an improvement on the agreement, because the Act had removed the situation whereby potential Sri Lankan citizens would be kept in suspense as to their status until the repatriation of the proportionate number of persons acquiring Indian citizenship. The difference between the Act and the Agreement is attributable to the fact that in 1965 the United National Party had won the elections with Dudley Senanayake installed as Prime Minister and the Act was introduced in Parliament during Dudley Senanayake's period, although the Agreement had been entered into by Sirimavo Bandaranaike.

On the 24th April 1968 both governments issued statements calling for applications and 30 April 1970 was fixed as the final date for the submission of applications. On the final date 700,000 persons had applied for Sri Lankan citizenship and 400,000 for Indian citizenship. Referring to the Agreement the Ceylon Workers Congress reported :

"Applying the ratio 7:4 for the grant of Indian and Ceylon citizenship on the basis of 700,000 (approx) applicants for Ceylon citizenship and 400,000 (approx) applicants for Indian citizenship it would be evident that only 225,000 (approx) applicants would be granted Ceylon citizenship leaving a balance of 475,000 (approx) together with their natural increase and those who may not have applied for either Ceylon or Indian citizenship under the Indo-Ceylon Agreement (Implementation) Act of 1967, aggregating over 600,000. There would, therefore, remain 600,000 stateless persons despite the implementation of the Indo-Ceylon Agreement (Implementation) Act"[9].

As would be observed, the total number of applicants for Sri Lanka and Indian citizenship exceeded the estimated number (975,000) by approximately 125,000. This number was not accounted for at the time of the agreement or subsequently.

Repatriation of persons granted Indian citizenship began in 1968. Mrs. Bandaranaike's Sri Lanka Freedom Party won the elections in 1970 and thereafter took steps to amend the Indo-Ceylon Agreement (Implementation) Act. The Indo-Ceylon Agreement (Implementation) (Amendment) Act of 1970 introduced the provision that four persons would be granted Sri

---

[9] Report of Activities   Ceylon Workers Congress, Oct. 1969 to Dec. 1971, Page 18

Lankan citizenship on the physical repatriation of seven persons to India.

In 1974 Sirimavo Bandaranaike and Indian Prime Minister Indira Gandhi entered into another agreement which in fact was supplementary to the 1964 agreement (27 January 1974). The fate of persons left over from the 1964 agreement was decided by this Agreement which equally divided the 150,000 persons between India and Sri Lanka. The present Jayewardene government amended the Indo-Ceylon Agreement (Implementation) Act once again in 1980 to revert to the old position of granting Sri Lankan citizenship to four persons once seven persons are recognised as Indian citizens.

But these agreements and legislation did not solve the problem of statelessness due to the reason that the governments were simply playing with numbers in order to proclaim that the problem had been solved, without taking any measure to ascertain the correctness of these numbers. As a result, in the beginning of 1986 there were nearly 500,000 stateless persons in Sri Lanka. Although the government of Sri Lanka in its earlier public statements mentioned only 93,000 stateless persons, later agreed that the number was close to 500,000.

In 1986, for the first time a significant demonstration took place over the citizenship issue. On the 3rd of December 1985 the National and Executive Councils of the Ceylon Workers Congress adopted a resolution declaring 1986 as the 'year of peace, amity and national reconciliation'. The Declaration further stated:

"One of the major stumbling blocks towards peace and harmony is statelessness and with this must be coupled the civic disabilities imposed on certain individuals for reasons outside ordinary law. Statelessness moreover is also a millstone around the necks of the Sinhalese plantation workers. Statelessness, a result of political victimisation, was legitimised over 35 years ago, and it must be removed forthwith for any real improvement in the lot of all plantation workers".[10]

The Councils of the Congress also decided to undertake various campaigns, the first of which was to observe the period from 14 January 1986 to 15 April 1986 (Thai Pongal festival day and Tamil-Sinhala New year day) as a 'period of meditation, prayer and meaningful preparation for the campaign to achieve national reconciliation through non-violence and peaceful dialogue'.

The words in the declaration such as 'Panchasila', 'Non-violence', 'Dharmista' and 'Prayer Campaign' did not however conceal the true nature of the declaration. There is little doubt that it was a notice for strike action given at the most suitable time. The government did not have room for manoeuvre because of the explosive situation in the north and east of the island and probably pressure brought about by the Indian government. Furthermore any strike action by the plantation workers would have had a devastating effect on the economy which was already collapsing. The government was unwillingly forced to grant citizenship to the stateless persons and the Grant of Citizenship to Stateless Persons Act was enacted. Prime Minister Premadasa speaking in Parliament on the Bill on 30th January 1986 announced the following statistics in relation to the Indo-Ceylon Agreements:

a) Sri Lankan Citizenship

1. Number of applicants	625,000
2. Number to be granted under agreements	375,000
3. Number granted	197,000
4. Natural increase granted	66,000
5. Number awaiting grant on ratio 7:4	43,153

---

[10] Congress News, May 1986, Vol.1 No.1

b) Indian Citizenship

1. Number of applicants	506,000
2. Number to be granted under agreements	600,000
3. Number granted	421,207
4. Natural increase granted	170,582
5. Number repatriated	337,066
6. Natural increase repatriated	123,835
7. Number granted and remaining in Sri Lanka	84,793

Under the Indo-Ceylon agreements of 1964 and 1974, 375,000 persons were to be granted Sri Lanka citizenship (300,000 + 75,000) and 600,000 Indian Citizenship (525,000 + 75,000). But only 506,000 had made application to the Indian High Commission for Indian citizenship. The balance 94,000 (600,000 − 506,000) who were to be granted Indian citizenship had in fact applied for Sri Lankan citizenship. The Grant of Citizenship to Stateless Persons Act No.5 of 1986 provided that these 94,000 would be granted Sri Lankan citizenship (section 1 clause 3). At the time of the Act 421,207 persons had been granted Indian citizenship and the Act stated that the Indian government had agreed to complete granting citizenship to the balance of 84,793 (506,000 − 421,207) persons within eight months of the Act (Section 1. clause 4).

Section 7 (1) provided that after grant of Sri Lankan citizenship to 469,000 (375,000 + 94,000) and Indian citizenship to 506,000 persons, any persons of Indian origin lawfully resident in Sri Lanka and is stateless, such person would be granted Sri Lankan citizenship.

The Act gives the impression of having solved the issue of statelessness. But the problem of implementation of the provisions of the Act remains and appears would remain for many more years to come. Despite the Sri Lankan Government agreeing to complete its part of the obligation within a period of 18 months, upto the end of 1986 only 32,000 persons, had been recommended for citizenship. After the lapse of 18 months since the enactment of the Act the Ceylon Workers Congress issued notice for another 'prayer campaign' in June 1987. The government which had slept over the implementation of the Act was rudely woken up, and it appears that officers are visiting each estate to complete the registration. The political situation in Sri Lanka is so volatile that the complete implementation of the provisions is doubtful. Furthermore, should the Sri Lanka Freedom Party (SLFP) form the next government there is grave doubt that the Act would remain in the statute books, as SLFP has already declared its opposition to the Act and the granting of citizenship to stateless persons. Nothing would prevent such a government from repealing the Act and declaring null and void any action taken under the Act.

Even if the Act is implemented fully, section 6 (1) has declared that the difference between citizenship by registration and citizenship by descent would remain. Section 5 (b) provides for the continuation of the issue of certificates of citizenship for those who are granted Sri Lankan citizenship. Therefore in future too the certificate of citizenship would be demanded as has been in the past, when a registered citizen transacts business, particularly with the government.

The 1972 Republican Constitution (effective from 22.5.72) did not include any provision on citizenship, and took away the existing rights of the minority communities by failing to incorporate a provision corresponding to Section 29 of the Soulbury Constitution which provided some measure of safeguard for the minorities. The draft Federal Constitution in the memorandum submitted to the Constituent Assembly by the (Tamil) Federal Party included a chapter on citizenship. But this memorandum and the memoranda submitted by the other representative Tamil organisations were ignored by the Constituent Assembly. The All-Ceylon Tamil Conference on the Constitution adopted a resolution on 5th February 1972 which read as follows:

"We regard it as a grave omission that no provision has been made in the Draft Constitution in regard to the conditions of citizenship and its acquisition; it is not enough to refer, in the section on the Franchise, to existing laws remaining in force. It is also unwholesome to divide citizens into categories and very discriminatory to imply that the National State Assembly can deprive any class of citizens of their status as citizenship."

Article 14 of the 1978 Constitution provides as follows:

14. (1) Every citizen in entitled to

a) the freedom of speech and expression including publication;

b) the freedom of peaceful assembly;

c) the freedom of association;

d) the freedom to form and join a trade union;

e) the freedom, either by himself or in association with others, and either in public or in private, to manifest his religion or belief in worship, observance, practice and teaching;

f) the freedom by himself or in association with others to enjoy and promote his own culture and to use his own language;

g) the freedom to engage by himself or in association with others in any lawful occupation, profession, trade, business or enterprise;

h) the freedom of movement and of choosing his residence within Sri Lanka; and

i) the freedom to return to Sri Lanka.

2) A person who, not being a citizen of any other country, has been permanently and legally resident in Sri Lanka immediately prior to the commencement of the Constitution and continues to be so resident shall be entitled, for a period of ten years from the commencement of the Constitution, to

the rights declared and recognised by paragraph (1) of this Article.

Paragraph (2) of this article provides that the persons, not being a citizen of any other country and who have been permanently and legally resident in Sri Lanka (this refers to the stateless persons) shall be entitled to fundamental rights recognized in paragraph (1).

This confirms the position prior to this constitution that the stateless Tamils were not entitled to fundamental rights specified in 14 (1) to which other citizens were entitled. Furthermore 14 (2) declared that the stateless persons will be entitled to fundamental rights only for a period of ten years (i.e. from 1978 February to 1988 February). This provision which grants fundamental rights to an entire community of people only for a period of ten years should shock the conscience of any person. But in Sri Lanka this is the order of the day.

The chapter on citizenship in the constitution declares that 'there shall be one status of citizenship of Sri Lanka (Article 26 (1)) and that a citizen of Sri Lanka shall for all purposes be described only as a "citizen of Sri Lanka", whether such person becomes entitled to citizenship by descent or by virtue of registration in accordance with the law relating to citizenship'. Superficially observed this provision purports to eliminate the distinction between citizens by registration and citizens by descent. But this is not the factual situation. Article 26 (4) ensures the continuation of the distinction between the two categories.

Article 15 of the Universal Declaration on Human Rights provides thus:

"Everyone has the right to a nationality"

"No one shall be arbitrarily deprived of his nationality nor denied the right to change his nationality"

Sri Lanka while continuing to remain a member of the United Nations and blatantly violating this article, unashamedly proceeded to ratify the International Covenants on Economic Social and Cultural Rights and Civil and Political Rights in 1980. It chose not to ratify the UN Convention on the Status of Stateless Persons or the Convention on the Reduction of Statelessness although there were nearly 500,000 stateless persons in the country.

In 1981 Sri Lanka proceeded further to celebrate the golden jubilee of the grant of the universal adult franchise (granted in 1931) on a grand scale without taking any measure for the reduction or elimination of statelessness.

3

EDUCATION

Although estate managements have shown little interest in the maintenance of schools for the children of plantation workers, a rudimentary form of education has been in existence on plantations, with Kanganies organising night schools for workers' children. The Rural Schools Ordinance No. 8 of 1907 provided for establishment of estate schools for children between the ages of 6 and 10. The superintendent was required to provide vernacular education and suitable school rooms under the Ordinance. The Ordinance No.1 of 1920 made it obligatory for the superintendent to appoint competent teachers and prohibited employment of children between the ages of 6 and 10 before 10 a.m. The part dealing with estate education in the Education Ordinance No.31 of 1939 was applicable only to estates having more that 25 children between the ages of 6 and 10. Under this Ordinance the Director of Education was empowered to make provision for broadening the scope of education in the estate schools. But this power does not seem to have been used.[11]

The Amendment Ordinance No.26 of 1947 converted all estate schools into primary state schools to form part of the system of national education. The amendment required the owner of the estate where there are over 27 children between the ages of 5 and 16 to provide suitable buildings for education but unlike the earlier provisions failed to make it obligatory on him to make provision for education of children or to appoint competent teachers. Further, although the estate schools

---

[11] Gnanamuttu, op.cit., Page 37

were purported to be within the educational system of the State, the Director of Education had no obligation under the Ordinance to establish or maintain schools on the estates. The Education Amendment Act No.5 of 1951 did not make any significant changes in the law relating to estate schools. It merely provided for legal action against the estate owner for failure to provide facilities required by the earlier Ordinance. Even this was vehemently opposed by the Planters' Association as being 'unduly heavy demand' of the Ordinance and due to this opposition the Minister of Education decided on 20th May 1953 to relax the implementation of the provisions relating to buildings for estate schools. Thus this provision although remaining in the statute-books became ineffective.

Under the Land Reform Law of 1972 and amendment of 1975 all estates were taken over by the State and are presently managed by the Janatha Estates Development Board (JEDB) and the Sri Lanka State Plantations Corporation (SLSPC). These being State Corporations, the responsibility of education of the estate children lies with the government. But both governments since 1975 have in fact worsened the position of estate schools. The Background Paper submitted at a seminar on 'Plantation youth and the economy of Sri Lanka', held by the CWC in Feb/March 1973 critisized the plantation education system:

"The educational facilities that are available to children of estate workers are a disgrace to a country which boasts of its free educational system. The curriculum of estate schools is hopelessly inadequate and compares most unfavourably with the primary schools in the rest of the island. The calibre of teachers in these estate schools is deplorable. Moreover most estate school buildings are in a dilapidated condition. To make matters worse, in 1962, a rule was introduced that in determining whether a school was Sinhala, Tamil or Muslim, non-citizens in the school should not be taken into consideration. As a result of this, a large number of schools in the plantation areas though they had a majority of Tamils became practically

Sinhalese or Muslim schools overnight".[12]

In 1987 the situation is no better than what it was in 1973. As a result of the discriminatory treatment meted out to the plantation Tamils, the literacy rate is lowest in the plantation sector. Table 1 shows the literacy rates in three sectors.

TABLE I

	URBAN	RURAL	ESTATE
LITERATE	88.7	84.3	61.2
ILLITERATE	11.3	15.7	38.8

SOURCE : SOCIO ECONOMIC SURVEY 1969/70

It was found in 1970 that 38.9% of the plantation population had no schooling, 51.0% had education upto primary level and only 1.3% had education upto GCE (Ordinary Level).[13] The position since then has deteriorated as the number of school children in estate schools had decreased from 74,376 in 1973 to 50,816 in 1976.

The poor education on plantations is connected to the plantation system as a whole. It is customary for children on estates to assist their parents in household chores, such as collection of firewood and cutting grass for livestock and to begin working at an early age in order to supplement the poor income of the parents. Although estates have schooling up to Grade 5 many drop out before that mainly due to economic reasons. Moreover the attitude of the plantation managements towards education of children is appalling. In the olden days the schools were conducted to keep the children occupied while parents were at work rather than providing meaningful education

---

[12] Background Paper, Page 8

[13] Socio Economic Survey 1969/70

and this may be true even today.[14]

When the Land Reform Commission took over the estates in 1972 some of the estates were distributed to villagers and the schools in these estates were closed. Where the school continued to exist, it may lie in the portion allocated to the villagers and the children resident on the former owner's allocation of land (The former owner of the estate was entitled to retain 50 acres of land under the Land Reform Law) did not have access to the school.

After the 1975 amendment to the Land Reform Law under which foreign owned estates were acquired by the State, the Education Department decided to take over schools and laid down certain conditions for such acquisition. Large number of schools which did not satisfy these conditions were left out.[15] Thereafter the government decided to take over all estate schools and reorganise the entire system under which many schools were closed without consultation with the trade unions or the parents. This resulted in many children being unable to attend school because of the distances involved. Teachers were sent for training under the scheme with UNICEF assistance without replacement causing disruption of the functioning of several schools.

Buildings provided by managements for schools are generally small and poorly ventilated and unfit for the conduct of classes. Only one building is usually provided by the estate without partition thereby compelling all five classes (Grades 1   5) to be held in the hall. Many schools are housed in half walled buildings adjoining a temple, creche, store-room or weighing shed, and some in lines or in buildings originally meant for

---

[14] Economic Review, March 1980. Vol.5 No.12   People's Bank Publication, Page 17

[15] ibid.

purposes other than schools.[16] Proper furniture is not provided for the schools. Long benches and tables are usually given and several children are made to sit on the benches in cramped conditions. Trained teachers are generally not available and in many schools one teacher is required to teach all five grades consisting of 50-100 children. The curriculum is totally inadequate and ranks extremely poor in comparison to other primary schools in the island. Very few teachers are appointed from within the plantation community itself. The atmosphere for education and learning is completely absent in these schools and governments have not allocated sufficient funds for any improvement.

Subsequent to the 1977 general elections 400 estate schools were taken over by the government and by 1980 all estate schools except 67 were brought under the Department of Education. Although this was a welcome move many schools were closed as a result of lack of teachers. The trade unions blamed the bureaucracy in the Education Department for creating such a condition.[17] Where Tamil streams were functioning in Sinhalese schools in the plantation areas, over the years the Tamil streams dried up or had their grades reduced. This policy of the government prompted the trade unions to call for separate schools for the Tamils in the plantation areas for secondary education.

The facilities for secondary education for children from the plantation are extremely poor. Few Tamil schools available are not offered proper assistance by the Department of Education and as in the case of the estate schools, these schools too have shortages of teachers, equipment and other necessaries and there is a total lack of teaching of science in these schools.

---

[16] Gnanamuttu, op.cit., Page 57

[17] Resolution No.8 adopted by the CWC   26th Convention, March 1979

Furthermore, as mentioned earlier governments placed many obstacles for the smooth functioning of these schools, such as converting the school to Sinhalese schools although the majority of the children are Tamil or abolishing Tamil streams thereby causing immense hardship to Tamil children who live in the vicinity in pursuing education.

It is not surprising in view of the above-mentioned reasons that very few children of the plantation workers enter the University. Even the little intake into universities from this community has been reduced since 1970 as a result of the introduction of standardisation. In 1970 the then government introduced a scheme of medium-wise standardisation the effect of which was that Tamil medium students were expected to score higher marks than the Sinhalese medium students. In addition to this scheme a district quota system was introduced in 1974 for alleged advancement of rural and underprivileged areas.[18] These schemes dealt a severe blow to the Tamils, including the plantation Tamils. A foremost authority on education in Sri Lanka C.R. de Silva states :

"However, it seems indisputable that the Indian Tamils who have by far the poorest schooling facilities in the island, were badly affected by standardistion. In 1970/71 when admissions were made on raw marks, eighteen Tamils of Indian origin entered the University of Ceylon, Peradeniya (Arts-12, Engineering-2, Medicine-1, Dental Surgery-1 and Science-2). In 1971/72 when marks were adjusted the number fell to twelve (Arts-8, Medicine-1, Dental Surgery-2, Agriculture-1) and with standardisation admissions to Peradeniya fell to eleven (Arts-7, Engineering-1, Dental Surgery-1, Agriculture-1). The district quota system seem to have had a slight beneficial effect in raising their admission to 13 in 1974 (Arts 10, Engineering and Science-2) but it may be noted that their admissions to Science-oriented

---

[18] For details see 'Discrimination in Education'   V Arumugam, Pages 48 - 72

courses seem to be steadily falling".[19]

After entering the university the problems of the plantation students are far from over. If he is a stateless person, he is required to pay a fee and is not entitled to receive loans from the bank like the other students. The parents of these students, being poor plantation workers would not be able to support them during their period of study and the student will not have any money to purchase books and equipment necessary for pursuance of his course of study. Fortunately some of the plantation trade unions have come to the aid of these students by providing them scholarships. Assistance has also been given by the 'Estate Education Trust', and in a few instances by philanthropists.

In 1987 the education facilities available to the plantation workers and their children remain as they were several decades ago without any improvement. At its 29th Convention the CWC in a resolution on Education noted that 'very little progress had been made in the filling of vacancies in the teaching staff and in providing educational facilities such as buildings, equipment and furniture for schools in the plantation sector' and deplored the 'total lack of facilities for teaching science in Tamil schools in estate areas' and called upon the Ministry of Education to 'remedy these serious drawbacks and shortcomings'.[20] But the government, as always remains unmoved.

It has to be pointed out that the plantation trade unions, though generally including educational facilities in their demands have failed to take concerted action in this important field. The trade unions have been conducting from the 1960s adult education seminars and courses by themselves or in collaboration

---

[19] 'Weightage in University Admissions, Standardisation and District Quota in Sri Lanka'   C R de Silva

[20] Resolution No.5 adopted by the CWC   29th Convention, March 1987

with the international trade union movement and the International Labour Organisation. But as regards basic education, trade unions seem to lack the enthusiasm which they show in other fields. It has been alleged, with some measure of truth, that the leaders of trade unions fear that a large cadre of educated youth in the plantations would undermine the power the trade unions have enjoyed for several decades. Whatever the reason may be, the trade unions must realise that the future of the plantation Tamils lies in education.

4

WAGES

The wages of the plantation workers have been extremely low in comparison to the other sectors of the economy, despite the fact that throughout the history of the plantations, this sector has been the major contributor to the national economy. A trade union writer has described the plantation labour as the 'heart that pumps the life-blood into the economic arteries of the country'. But this important sector has always been discriminated against in all aspects of national life, including payment of wages.

Wages Boards established under the Wages Boards Ordinance No.7 of 1941 determine the minimum wages comprising (i) a basic wage and (ii) a Cost of Living Allowance for the Tea and Rubber growing and manufacturing trades. The quorum for the meeting of the Wages Board is six, consisting of the Commissioner of Labour (or Assistant Commissioner or Deputy Commissioner), a nominated member and four representative members of whom two will have to be employer representatives and two worker representatives (section 11 (i)). Therefore the worker representatives would always be in the minority and it is extremely difficult to make changes in basic wage levels.

The minimum daily wage rate for a male tea estate worker in 1955 was Rupees 2.06 and in 1980 it was Rupees 2.51. This shows that the change in the basic wage has been insignificant although allowances have increased over the years. Ron Rote writing on the wage levels of plantation workers states:

"Although minimum wages for the industry have been fixed since 1945, the actual minimum has always been far below the national average. In 1972, for instance the daily rate for tea workers was Rs. 2.87 whereas an unskilled engineering worker earned Rs.6.25: Between 1955 and 1968 tea workers had an increase in wage rates of only 27 percent, while unskilled government workers had an increase of 63.4 percent and the same category of engineering trade had 90.6 percent"[21].

The plantation workers are paid wages at a daily rate although wages are paid monthly. Section ⟩ (2) of the Estate Labour (Indian) Ordinance provided :

"Where wages are payable at a daily rate, the monthly wages shall be computed according to the number of days on which the labourer was able and willing to work and actually demanded employment, whether the employer was or was not able to provide him work :

Provided that an employer shall not be bound to provide for any labourer more than six days' work in the week".

Although this provision is in force for several decades it is not adhered to by the plantation managements. Where the worker is willing and able to work but is not offered work for a day, he is not paid any wages for that day, despite the law laying down specifically that he should be paid. However high the daily wage rate increases may be (such is not the actual case) the total monthly wage will always be low because of the fact that the work offered per week is generally three to four days a week or even less. The following table shows the average number of days work offered in a month:

[21] 'A Taste of Bitterness - The Political Economy of Tea Plantations in Sri Lanka' - Ron Rote, Page 85

44

TABLE II

AVERAGE NUMBER OF DAYS OF WORK
OFFERED PER MONTH

	1971		1972		1973		1974		1975		1976	
	Days (Mar.)	Days (Sep.)	Days (Mar.)	Days (Sep.)	Days (Mar.)	Days (Sep.)	Days (Mar.)	Days (Sep.)	Days (Mar.)	Days (Sep.)	Days (Mar.)	Days (Sep.)
M ...	6.6	6.1	4.9	5.5	5.6	5.1	4.9	5.7	6.4	6.1	5.5	6.0
F ...	6.8	6.3	5.0	5.6	5.8	5.6	5.8	5.7	6.8	5.4	5.2	5.8
C.M ...	5.3	4.4	6.1	5.0	4.4	5.4	5.8	3.7	7.3	5.4	3.4	6.6
C.F ...	6.0	4.8	4.6	4.4	4.4	6.1	5.7	4.2	5.7	4.8	3.7	5.5

CM   Children Male

CF   Children Female

Source: Statistical Abstracts 1976
Reproduced by Economic Review
Vol.5 No.1

Economic Review pointed out that the number of working days for a month was "alarmingly low" 22%. The Government made regulations in March 1974 (Emergency (Estate Workers' Guaranteed Minimum Wage) Regulation .No. 1 of 1974), to compel managements to provide work for a minimum of 109 days in every six months and in 1975 the managements were required to offer 120 days in six months. But the regulation did not provide for minimum number of days of work per week and therefore it was possible for workers to be out of work for several weeks. The employers could offer work during the main seasons and not offer work at all during other time and still be within the requirement of the regulations. Successive governments chose to turn a blind eye to the non-implementation of the provision of the Estate Labour (Indian) Ordinance and misled the public by taking other measures ignoring the provision. One such instance was when the plantation manage-

---

[22] Economic Review, op.cit., Page 14

ments (controlled by the government) announced the offer of six days work a week, when trade unions were poised for strike action in 1984. This completely misled the international trade union movement and the media into thinking that this was a new generous offer by the government.

At the time of the strike by the plantation trade unions in April 1984, the basic wages per day prescribed for Tea and Rubber Growing and Manufacturing Trades were as given in the following Table:

TABLE III

	Male	Female	Child
Tea	Rs.4.51	Rs.4.32	Rs.4.07
Rubber	2.65	2.55	2.30

In 1970 the Ceylon Workers Congress had entered into a collective agreement with the Ceylon Estates Employers Federation (CEEF) for a wage supplement to workers on rubber estates based on the average sale price of RSS No.1. rubber grade. The provisions of this collective agreement were extended by the Minister under the Industrial Disputes Act to all rubber estates of over 100 acres, in January 1975. A similar price wage supplement was also offered by the government in 1975 for tea estate workers, based on the nett sale average of midgrown teas. In 1975 the price wage supplement for tea was as follows:-

TABLE IV

Average nett sale price	Price wage supplement
Rs.2.50 2.74	10 cts per worker per day
Rs.2.75 2.99	20 cts per worker per day
Rs.3.00 and over	30 cts per worker per day

If these had been continued the plantation workers would have received substantial increases in wages. However the government intervened and froze the price-wage supplement for workers on tea estates in 1979 at the nett sale average of midgrown teas in 1975. The price wage supplement for the workers on rubber estates was frozen at the price of RSS No.1 in November 1977.

In June 1982 the Wages Board for Tea Growing and Manufacturing Trade decided to grant an increase in the cost of living allowance. But this decision was not approved by the government (For implementation of the wages boards decision the approval of the Minister is necessary). If the decision had been implemented, in 1984 plantation workers would have received a cost of living allowance of Rupees 15.85 per day in relation to the cost of living index of 542.1 at that time, instead of Rupees 8.42 per day. Furthermore had the price wage supplement not been frozen by the government in 1984 the tea workers would have received a price wage supplement of Rupees 9.90 per day instead of -/30 cents per day based on the nett sale average of midgrown teas at Rupees 60/- per kilogram. Adding these entitlements the tea worker on an estate not less than 100 acres, in 1984, would have received Rupees 35/31 instead of Rupees 18/28 paid at that time.[23]

Between 1968 and 1984 several laws were enacted to grant cost of living allowances to workers in Sri Lanka. Every one of these legislations was discriminatory as far as the plantation workers were concerned, although these workers were in a worse position than other workers in the country by reason of the low wages and their position as daily paid workers. The following table shows the discrimination in the payment of allowances:

---

[23] Plantation Strike 1984   CWC publication

TABLE V

NAME OF   AMOUNT GRANTED
ALLOWANCE

	PLANTATION LABOUR	OTHER SECTORS
Interim Devaluation Allowance 1968	30 Cents per day	40 cents per day
Cost of living Allowance-1972	Males 18 cents per day	Shortfall of salary of Rupees 180/- per month
	Females) Children) 12 cents per day	Minimum of Rupees 7/50 (approximately 29 cents per day
Private sector	10% or Rupees 20 whichever is less, but frozen at the 1975 wage level	10% or Rupees 20 whichever is less
Supplementary	Rupees 2/50 per day	Rupees 2/50 per day
Allowance 1979	Rupees 3/52 per day as Col allowance but frozen at Col index 245.9 (by 1984 the i.e. 542.1 Col index had risen to 542.1)	Col Allowance based on cost of living index in 1984
Allowance 1980	Nil	Rupees 70/- per month
Consolidation of wages 1982	Nil	Basic wage and special allowance consolidated with consequential increase in statutory dues
Cost of living Allowance 1982	Nil	Rupees 100 per month
Computation of Col Allowance 1982	3 cents per day for increase of every point in the Col index (i.e. 78 cents per month)	Rupees 2 for increase of every point in the Col index
Cost of living allowance 1984	Nil	Rupees 102/- per month effective from 1.3.1984

SOURCE: Plantations Strike 1984   CWC

Governments, in order to increase the volume of domestic capital have imposed heavy taxation on tea which has resulted in the deprivation of investment in the plantation sector. The extraction of surplus in the sector was made possible by keeping the wages at a low level and depriving the plantation sector of the wage increases granted to other sectors. Such measures by the present government have been criticised by observers as ethnically motivated. P. Devaraj and M. Sinnathamby in their note on 'Developments in the Plantation Sector 1977-1983' argue that 'this was possible for the government since the large majority of the estate workers belonged to an ethnic minority' and point out that 'the plantation workers had always been subjected to much exploitation and oppression and this exploitation was further intensified during the period of the present government'.

From Table VI it would be noted that there had been a sharp rise in the wages between 1977 and 1984 from Rs.8.61 to Rs.16.69. Although money wages had increased sharply real wages have shown a decline after 1979. The decrease is from Rs.4.40 in 1979 to Rs.3.08 in 1984 (March). If we compare the real wages in 1977 and 1984, both are almost the same while the cost of living has risen sharply.

Regarding the calculation of real wages of plantation workers, Sinnathamby states:

"For a realistic calculation of real wages of plantation workers. ..... it is the COL index relating to food items that is the most appropriate since they spend nearly 70% of their earnings on food. When this is done the fall in real wages after 1979 is very much sharper. In 1983 it stood at Rs.3.18 which was lower than the 1978 level".[24]

---

[24] The April Strike of the Plantation Workers (Part 2)   M Sinnathamby, Lanka Guardian, 1.8.84

Sinnnathamby noted that similar trends were reflected in monthly earnings of the plantation workers as shown in Table VII.

TABLE VI

Wages of Tea Estate Workers
COL Index (1952=100) Real wages in terms of

Year	Daily Wages	All Items	Food Items	All Items	Food Items
1975	5.06	198.3	204.3	2.55	2.48
1976	5.92	200.7	202.1	2.95	2.93
1977	6.17	203.2	203.3	3.04	3.03
1978	8.61	227.8	237.5	3.78	3.63
1979	11.10	252.3	263.3	4.40	4.42
1980	12.87	318.2	339.7	4.04	3.79
1981	12.87	315.4	399.6	3.43	3.22
1982	14.95	416.1	450.4	3.83	3.32
1983	16.08	474.2	506.3	3.39	3.18
1984	16.69	542.2	553.2	3.08	2.91

TABLE VII

Average Monthly Earnings of Tea Estate Workers
Col Index (1952=100)   Real Earnings (Rs/Cts) in terms of

Year	Monthly Earnings	All Items	Food Items	All Items	Food Items
1975	100.45	198.3	204.3	50.43	49.17
1976	99.85	200.7	202.1	49.75	49.40
1977	132.11	203.2	203.3	65.01	64.98
1978	166.95	227.8	237.5	73.29	70.29
1979	218.09	252.3	263.3	86.48	82.86
1980	239.42	318.2	339.7	75.24	70.48
1981	229.63	375.4	399.6	61.17	57.46
1982	285.79	417.1	450.4	69.10	63.45

Before 1977 all plantation workers were issued subsidised rice but in 1977 this was withdrawn in respect of most of the workers based on the poverty line fixed at Rs.300/-. Although the prices were rising rapidly each year, over the years this unrealistic poverty line remained the same thus affecting the vast majority of the plantation workers depriving them of the subsidy.

Moreover, female workers were being paid less than the male workers in contravention of the ILO conventions on employment to which the Sri Lanka is a signatory.

All the reasons stated above prompted the CWC to issue notice on the employers (Janatha Estates Development Board and Sri Lanka State Plantations Corporation) in May 1983 to correct the anomalies in the wages of the plantation workers. The State corporation and the government ignored the notice and refused to negotiate and therefore the CWC decided on 12th February 1984 to resort to strike action if the demands were not met within a month. The CWC also called upon the other plantation unions to join the strike and there was unprecedented solidarity amongst the trade unions. Fourteen trade unions in the membership of the Joint Plantation Trade Union Committee and the Lanka Jathika Estate Workers Union (LJEWU) which is a union with political affiliation to the government party, offered support for the decision. The wages of tea and rubber workers before the strike were as follows:

TABLE VIII

	Male	Female
Tea growing	18.43	15.31
Rubber growing	20.18	17.21

One week before the strike the government intervened and agreed to implement the following proposals made by the JEDB in consulation with M/S Ernst & Winney (consultants) :

TABLE IX

	Male	Female
Tea growing	20.51	20.51
Rubber growing	20.76	20.76

SOURCE: The April Strike of the Plantation Workers - M. Sinnathamby - Part 1 - Lanka Guardian 15.7.84

The LJEWU accepted this offer and withdrew from the strike. The other unions joined the strike and it was notable that even the members of the LJEWU stayed away from work in spite of the advise of their leaders and the concerted compaign against the strike by the Sri Lankan media. The strike lasted for nine days from 1st April 1984 and the employers and the government caved in. The following demands by the workers were met:

1) Wage increase - Rs.23.75 per day (male and female workers).
2) Equal wages for male and female workers.
3) Assurance of six days work in a week.
4) Appointment of a Committee to consider further wage increase.

Despite the assurance of offer of 6 days work a week, many estates do not offer such work, nor do the estates pay wages, where the worker offers himself for work, as required by law. Further the Committee that was appointed to study wage increases and other demands has not thus far made any recommendations. Therefore as far as wages of the plantation workers are concerned, the old story continues.

In relation to wages and other payments the plantation workers are discriminated against in comparison to workers in other sectors. The Tea and Rubber Growing and Manufacturing Trade Wages Boards have declared only two days as public holidays for the entire year, although these Wages Boards are entitled to declare a maximum of 9 days as holidays, while in majority of the other trades nine days have been declared. The plantation workers are entitled to receipt of wages without work for the May Day and the April New Year day (ie. Day off with pay or double the rate for eight hours and treble the rate for in excess).

In the computation of overtime rates for plantation workers daily rate is taken as the basis for computation with additional pay of 25% per hour for work between 7 am and 7 pm and 50% per hour for work between 7 pm and 7 am. But in majority of other trades for which Wages Boards have been established, the basis for computation is the monthly rate with 50% per hour for work at any time throughout the day.

In the case of computation of payment for work on weekly holiday, similar method is adopted. In some of the trades the worker is entitled in addition to payment of wages, a day off in lieu of the day he has worked. The plantation trade workers are not entitled to such additional holiday.[25]

The plantation workers remain the lowest paid and the worst discriminated lot while making the highest contribution to the economy by their toil. Sri Lanka has immensely benefitted by the plantation sector and several welfare measures this century for the whole country have been made possible by this sector. Table X shows the export earnings of tea:

TABLE X

	1950	1960	1970	1980	1983
AREA UNDER TEA (1000 ACRES)	567.4	581.8	597.5	604.4	598.1
TEA PRODUCED (1000 METRIC TONS)	143.7	197.6	212.2	191.4	179.3
TEA EARNINGS (RUPEES MILLIONS)	752	1,096	1,116	6,170	8,295

SOURCE: CENTRAL BANK REPORTS

25 'Wages, Terms and Conditions of Employment in Sri Lanka' P Navaratne

5

HOUSING AND HEALTH

HOUSING

Most of the plantation workers live in barrack-like 'line-rooms' (90-100 feet by 15 feet). Each line room is 10 feet by 12 feet in extent. A few line rooms have common verandahs. Most of the line room were built 60 years ago and are in a dilapidated condition. The Socio-Economic Survey of 1969/70 showed that 1,170,700 (89%) plantation workers occupied 225, 720 units of line rooms, thus the occupancy rate at that time was 5.1. The same survey showed this type of single room accomodation was found only in the estate sector while in the rural and urban sectors majority of the housing units had two to three rooms.

The entire family of the worker cooks, eats and sleeps in this one room, irrespective of the number of members of the family. The Estate Labour (Indian) Ordinance of 1889 (Section 24 (1)) requires the management of the estate to provide a separate room for each married couple and a child under the age of 12 years. It is common for managements to ignore such provision often resulting in three generations of a family living in the same room. The managements have compelled, on several occasions, two or three different families to live in one line room. In 1973 War on Want found that in an estate in Nuwara Eliya as many as 30 families were living in lines huddled and congested into 14 rooms.[26] Consumer Finances

---

[26] 'The State of Tea'   Edith M. Bond

Survey in 1973 showed that over crowding (defined as more than two persons per room) in the plantation sector was 75% while in urban and rural areas it was 35% and 37% respectively.[27] Despite continued agitation by trade unions at local level, repairs to line rooms are almost never done. This has resulted in walls cracking and roofs leaking thereby contributing to the poor health conditions of the workers. Very few line rooms have latrines close by and these almost always are without water supply.

The construction of line rooms was prohibited in 1950 under Rules made in terms of Section 12 of the Diseases (Labourers) Ordinance of 1912 and in the subsequent years several plans were made by the government to improve accommodation of the workers.[28] These plans were never implemented. Plantations have been excluded from National Housing Schemes such as the Million Houses Programme, Self Help Housing Schemes and Gam Udawa Programmes. It is an appalling state of affairs; whereas 1987 has been declared by the United Nations as the International Year of Shelter for the Homeless (IYSH) on a proposal made by the Prime Minister of Sri Lanka R. Premadasa and construction of million houses are planned in Sri Lanka, the most needy section of the population has been ignored by the government, to live and suffer in the same 'old' line rooms.

International organisations have assisted in a limited way for the improvement of housing on estates. These projects are Netherlands Assistance Programme for cottage type housing (25 estates), World Bank Tree Crop Rehabilitation Project housing components (for 100 estates) and the UNICEF Programme (begun in 1984 for 17 estates). These attempts are totally inadequate in view of the enormity of the requirement

---

[27] Economic Review, op.cit., Page 15

[28] Gazette No. 10168 of 27.10.1950.

for improvement in housing on the plantations. The following report confirms this position :

"However up until now, those projects have had little impact on the overall housing conditions on plantations. It has been estimated that about 250,000 housing units under the two estate corporations, JEDB and SLSPC require upgrading and renovation".[29]

HEALTH

The Country Statement submitted by Sri Lanka at the Third Asian and Pacific Population Conference in 1982 states that 'Sri Lanka provides extensive health care for the entire population through well organised primary health care scheme'.[30] This is an absolutely false statement, in that the plantation workers are discriminated once again in the provision of health facilities.

The Medical Wants Ordinance No.9 of 1912 though providing for the medical wants of the plantation workers failed to impose legal obligation on the managements to provide medical facilities and to provide for sick pay for workers. If a worker is sick and is unable to work he would lose his wages for the days he does not report for work as result of the illness.

Generally one dispensary serves several estates and there are no hospitals on estates. The Medical Assistant in the dispensary is inadequately qualified and sometimes resorts to illegal practices by selling the drugs and demanding money from the workers. Because of shortage of drugs the Medical Assistants find it extremely difficult to care for the sick. If a plantation worker

---

[29] 'Plantations and Plantation Workers'   Jean-Paul Sajhau and Jurgen Von Muralt, Page 158

[30] The Conference was held in Colombo from 20th to 29th September, 1982

is to be admitted to the general hospital he has to obtain a note from the superintendent without which he will not be admitted. The estate will have to pay the hospital for the number of days he remains there. Due to this reason superintendents often refuse to issue the note unless the condition of the worker is very serious. Moreover although the sick worker is entitled to be provided transport to the hospital more often than not such transport is denied by the managements.

Maternity facilities on estates are inadequate. Due to this reason child birth takes place often in the line rooms. United Front for Repatriate Workers describes the problem in the following manner:

"Estates in which there are no maternity wards, there are many such estates, child birth takes place in the congested, ill-ventilated and dirty line rooms of the workers. Such births are often attended by illiterate and retired old women whose methods are crude and highly life risky. Nursing mothers are not given proper advice on diet and child care and as a result child and mother are exposed to score of diseases".[31]

Due to these reasons and the poor health of women workers maternal and infant mortality rates are very high in the plantation sector as Table XI shows: (page 57)

In 1979 the infant mortality rate in the plantation sector was 110 per thousand while in the urban and rural areas it was 44.7 and 24.6 respectively.

The Economic Review speaking of the health conditions of the plantation areas states:

"A WHO study on the distribution of health facilities..... revealed that health facilities in these areas were far below the

---

[31] Report of Activities   UFRW, December 1984, Page 21

national averages. Doctors per 100,000 of the population was 15.2, 13.2 and 13.4 for the Central, Uva and Sabaragamuwa provinces compared to a national average of 25.7. Similarly nurses per 100,000 of the population was 29.5, 24.1 and 34.6 for the same three provinces while the all-island figure was 50.8".[32]

TABLE XI

Mortality Rates: Major Plantation Districts
(per 1,000 live births)

	1950	1955	1960	1965	1970	1972	1974	1976	1978
1. Infant Morality Rates									
N'Eliya	108	106	83	85	90	84	119	100	75
Badulla	90	75	63	63	59	59	73	51	47
Kandy	92	86	70	66	64	66	92	61	60
Average: 3 districts	96	89	72	72	71	70	95	71	61
Average: Sri Lanka	84	70	57	54	47	46	51	44	37
2. Maternal Mortality Rates									
N'Eliya	5.6	4.4	4.0	3.4	2.9				
Badulla	6.8	4.2	3.5	2.4	1.9				
Kandy	6.9	4.8	3.8	3.8	2.1				
Average: 3 districts	6.4	5.9	3.8	3.2	2.3				
Average: Sri Lanka	6.4	4.2	3.2	2.3	1.5				

Note: Multi-year averages 1950-1972
Sources: Administration Reports of the Registrar General
Statistical Abstracts of Ceylon, 1982
W.N.A. Fernando (1980a: 165-167)

(Table taken from 'A Taste of Bitterness'   Ron Rote   page 86)

The plantation workers, as a result of poor health conditions, poor accommodation and the cold climatic conditions suffer from a variety of diseases.

Rachel Kurian visiting estates in 1980/81 found that the most frequent illnesses were bowel disorders, stomach pains and

---

[32] Economic Review, op.cit., Page 16

stomach trouble (associated with bad drinking water and inadequate sanitary conditions), boils, fever and headache. In the colder areas coughs, chest pains, shivering and difficulties in breathing were also reported.[33]

Kumari Jayawardene attributes the reason for higher incidence of disease on plantation to malnutrition and states that stunting among children is another serious problem.[34] Malnutrition also causes increase in infant mortality rates. The Sri Lankan Nutrition Survey of 1976 showed that in the estate sector only 35% of children between 6-7 months were normal as against 65.8% in the villages. Table XII shows that stunting and wasting amongst plantation children are high.

TABLE XII

PERCENTAGE DISTRIBUTION OF CHILDREN 6 - 7 MONTHS OF AGE BY WATER-LOW 1975/76

POPULATION	NORMAL	STUNTING	WASTING	WASTING/ STUNTING
Total				
Sri Lanka	62.0	31.4	3.3	3.4
Village	65.8	27.8	3.4	3.0
Estate	35.0	56.3	3.6	6.1

Source: Sri Lanka Nutrition Status Survey 1976

On the whole, the health scene on the plantation is appalling and the government has taken insignificant measures to remedy this enormous problem. It is to the credit of the plantation Tamil worker that he continues to produce as always for the survival of the country in such pitiful health conditions, which exploiters do not seem to appreciate. It is sheer hypocricy for the government to claim at an international forum that extensive health care is provided to all people in Sri Lanka.

---

[33]'The Position of Women Workers in the plantation Sector in Sri Lanka' - Rachel Kurian, ILO, 1981

[34] Recent Changes in the Welfare of Children and Women in the Plantation Sector - Kumari Jayawardena, World Development, 12.3.84. Extracts in Voice of the Voiceless, No.22 September 1985

6

VIOLENCE AGAINST THE PLANTATION TAMILS

Violence has been continuously perpetrated against the plantation Tamils particularly since 1970 after Sirimavo Bandaranaike's government swept into power. Violence is directed against them as Tamils and as ordinary workers. In the early 1956 and 1958 violences against the Tamils, the plantation Tamils were mostly spared, although Tamils of Indian origin living in other areas were subject to physical violence.

Physical violence is also meted out to them as individuals. The superintendents and the supervisory staff, who are now mainly Sinhalese, behave like masters having absolute power over slaves and have no qualms assaulting the workers. The majority of the strikes in the plantation areas are due to physical violence against workers. Complaints to the police may cause further harassment; the only protection they seek is from trade unions and by trade union action. On many occasions the trade unions themselves are helpless with the entire government machinery working against the workers. Economic Review of March 1980 States as follows :

"In addition, strikes due to questions arising out of transfer of workers from one estate to another or the high-handed and illegal acts like assault on workers, looting, house breaking, thuggery by staff and superintendents have also been issues that have provoked strikes"[35].

---

[35] Economic Review, op.cit., Page 10

The police has continued to harass the workers and on several occasions resorted to murder, but have always escaped the consequences. The Report of Activities of the Ceylon Workers Congress (CWC) for the period October 1969 to December 1971 described the situation on the plantations as follows :

"We have to record with considerable concern the surfacing of a dangerous trend in the Labour Management relations on the plantations where certain employers by themselves or with the active support of the Police are seeking to silence the workers from obtaining their just demands at gun point. Apart from the death toll that has punctuated the industrial scene in this sector of the economy over the last thirty years, recent incidents of the shooting down of estate workers by the Police and certain managements have shown a dangerous increase as evidenced by the death of seven plantation workers during the period under review".

In the same report the CWC condemned police atrocities on Mayfield estate, Meddecombra estate, Dunsinane estate, Kellabokka estate and Galaha estate and called upon the government to "circumscribe the limits of police authority to ensure the legitimate rights of the workers". But the government failed to take suitable action.

THE PERIOD BETWEEN 1970 AND 1977

This period witnessed organised mob violence against the plantation Tamils, particularly after the enactment of the Land Reform Law. Under the Land Reform Law No.1 of 1972 landholdings in excess of 50 acres were vested in the Land Reform Commission on the appointed date (back dated to 29 May 1971). An amendment to the Land Reform Law in 1975 brought the foreign company owned estates under the Land Reform Commission.

Politicians belonging to the SLFP declared in their speeches in Parliament and outside that lands taken away from the Sinhalese peasants by the foreigners more than hundred years ago had been restored to them by the Land Reform Law. Minister of Lands, Kobbekaduwa himself headed the crusade and denounced the plantation Tamils and their leaders in Parliament. In every speech outside Parliament he made it a point to attack the plantation Tamils so that resentment among the Sinhalese population reached fever pitch. On the day of the enactment of the Land Reform Law, Members of Parliament led thugs to plantation areas and began assaulting every worker who was sighted.

Line rooms were attacked and meagre possessions of the plantation Tamils were looted by the mobs. The member of Parliament for Gampola, W.M. Jayaratne was vociferous in his verbal attacks and participated in the physical attacks on the plantation Tamils.

The physical abuse of the plantation Tamils was worsened by the food shortage that was prevalent in the island between 1972 and 1975 due "austerity" measures of the government. The plantations were badly affected by the food shortage. The shortage was so acute that many persons, particularly old men and women died of starvation. As a result the rate of natural increase (per 1000 population) dropped from 14.0 in 1973 to 7.1 in 1974 for the Tamils of Indian origin, whereas the drop for all other ethnic groups was from 20.3 in 1973 to 18.5 in 1974.[36] (For death rates see Table XV in Appendix)

During these years one was able to observe plantation workers flocking in nearby towns to sell their few properties or to beg in the streets. Even at this pathetic stage, traders resorted to exploitation and politicians attempted to make political capital

---

[36] ibid., Page 16

out of their sufferings. (The writer observed a senior Sinhalese member of the present cabinet, then in opposition, leading a miserable batch of Tamil workers on the streets of Nuwara Eliya and making them shout political slogans).

Part of the land acquired under the Land Reform Law was distributed among the Sinhalese political supporters of the SLFP. These persons who came to reside on the plantations continued their harassment of the plantation Tamils throughout the period the SLFP government was in power. The worst of the violence during the period took place in 1976 against Tamil workers of Delta and Sanguhar estates in the Gampola District. Once again the MP for Gampola, W.M. Jayaratne led these attacks. Scores of thugs descended upon these estates with an assortment of weapons, dragged the workers out of their line rooms, including women and children, and brutally assaulted them. Many workers were seriously injured. Then the thugs proceeded to kill the livestock on the estate and burn the line rooms. The government, without taking any action against the offenders and failing to provide any assistance for the rehabilitation of the workers, attempted to take measures to distribute the two estates and 10,000 acres of land surrounding these estates to Sinhalese persons. But this time, the workers were ready and prevented the surveying of the land for distribution. The police arrived at the scene and when the workers refused to withdraw, opened fire killing a young worker named Sivanu Letchumanan. As a result of the killing the workers in all the estates in the hill country struck work and the government conceded defeat by revoking the order for distribution of land.

In his evidence before the Sansoni Commission M. Subbiah a trade union officer referred to the attack on plantation workers :

"In March 1976 Choisy Estate, Punduloya, was attacked by outsiders claiming to be a committee headed by Mr. Weerasekera, MP for Kotmale. The workers were chased out of the estate, and the committee divided the estate calling themselves People's Committee. The same fate overtook the workers of Balapokuna estate.... The workers were similarly ousted from Dartry and Orion Estates in the Gampola district and from Moolgama estate. In May 1976 workers were ousted from Sanguhar and Delta Estates, the object being to distribute those estates among Sinhalese colonists. Other estates where workers were treated in the same lawless manner were.... Uduwela in Kandy and Karandupona in Kegalle".[37]

THE 1977 GENOCIDAL MASSACRE

From the 13th of August 1977 several incidents took place in Jaffna in which policemen assaulted members of the public and burnt and damaged property. Even the leader of the Opposition A. Amirthalingam was assaulted by the police. On 17 August 1977 the police sent a false radio message to Colombo informing that the Naga Vihare (Buddhist shrine on the island of Nainativu off the Jaffna peninsula) had been attacked and that the Jaffna people were gathering at the railway station to attack in-coming passengers. This false information spread like wild fire kindling racial hatred and violence in the South of the island. The Sansoni Commission described the message as follows :-

"It was sent with mischievous intent, and could have created an ugly situation. The usual spate of rumours began, and exaggeration playing its part as the rumours spread from mouth to mouth."[38]

President Jayewardene added fuel to fire by challenging the Tamils in a statement in Parliament on 18 August 1977 : "If you want to fight, let there be a fight; if it is peace, let there be peace."

---

[37] Sansoni Commission Report, Page

[38] ibid., Page 104 paragraph 105

Violence spread to the entire country. Plantation areas were widely affected, including estates, towns and villages. Tamils were massacred in their hundreds and Tamil property was looted, burnt or otherwise destroyed. It was estimated that between 5,000 to 7,500 families besides being subjected to bodily injury and in some cases rape and murder, lost all or nearly all goods they possessed because of the cruel attacks on the plantation population.[39]

Evidence was provided before the Sansoni Commission relating to attacks on Tamil plantation workers on estates in Ratnapura, Kiriella, Neboda, Matugama, Galle, Haputale, Bandarawela, Kandy, Panwila, Teldeniya, Matale, Elkaduwa, Kurunegala, Kegalle, Hewahette, Galaha, Kadugannawa, Hangurankette, Deltota, Rikillagaskada, Ulapane and Dolosbage.[40] Evidence included burning of line rooms, temples and houses, assault, looting, rape, murder and injury. Evidence was also provided on attacks on Tamil shops and Tamil people in the towns in the plantation areas.

Nearly 500 Tamils were killed in the August 1977 violence and property worth millions of rupees was destroyed and during the violence, the police either failed to take action or arrived too late to prevent death and destruction. On several occasions they even refused to take action. When a Tamil reported the murder of his father-in-law to the Matugama police they responded: "When our Police officers were murdered in Jaffna, what is the harm in your people being murdered."[41] The Sansoni Commission which was appointed by the President of Sri Lanka on 9th November 1977 to inquire into the August 1977 incidents agreed that 'the law enforcement machinery of the State, and in particular the Police, by and large failed to

---

[39] Coordinating Secretariat for Plantation Areas, Kandy.

[40] Sansoni Commission Report, Pages 133-143 and 192-237

[41] ibid., Page 41

discharge its function of protecting the vicitims and preventing the incidents.'[42]

The physical and psychological suffering of the plantation Tamils as a result of the violence was immense. After the violence there was no rehabilitation programme to speak of, by the government, despite receiving substantial aid from foreign countries and the people affected languished for many months in refugee camps. The Memorandum of the Tamil Rescue Appeal to the UN Commission on Human Rights described the plight of the plantation Tamils:

"The worst affected section of the Tamils was the most vulnerable plantation Tamils. Thousands of them were attacked by marauding mobs of hooligans in their plantations, their line rooms and the streets. They were beaten up and many were killed. They were relieved of their pitifully little worldly possessions. School halls and church halls were filled with thousands of plantation Tamil refugees. Many ran into the jungle and hid themselves for weeks and others trekked towards the Tamil areas of the north and east seeking safety".[43]

The Sansoni Commision recommended, among others, that the Tamils affected should be compensated by the State adequately for their loss. Although the terms of reference, required the Commission to recommend measures as may be necessary to rehabilitate or assist in any other manner the persons affected, the recommendations of the Commission were ignored by the government.

THE 1981 GENOCIDAL MASSACRE

In August 1981, another widespread organised violence was perpetrated against the Tamils, particularly the plantation Tamils

---

[42] ibid., Page 266

[43] Memorandum by the Tamil Rescue Appeal to the UN Commission on Human Rights, paragraph 186

in the Sabaragamuwa Province. The violence began in Amparai and an altercation between Sinhalese and Tamil students Anti-Tamil feeling among the Sinhalese had been raised to a state of frenzy by speeches made by politicians in Parliament, particularly those of government M.P. Dr. Neville Fernando and Cyril Mathew, Minister of Industries. Cyril Mathew had, at this stage published a book entitled "Sinhala People, Arise and Safeguard Buddhism", containing 352 pages of anti-Tamil propaganda. The situation was made worse by the no-confidence motion moved by government MPs in parliament against the leader of the Opposition A. Amirthalingam.

Although Tamils were attacked everywhere, the attacks were severe in the Ratnapura District in the Sabaragamuwa province. Gangs of thugs with weapons arrived in state-owned buses to Kahawatta, Rakwana, Nivitigala, Pelmadulla, Balangoda and other areas in the district and entered estates to seek out Tamil plantation workers. They also went into towns to attack Tamils and Tamil-owned shops. The Tamils became victims of mass murder, rape and assault. Tamil property was looted and line rooms, shops and houses were burnt. In all 43 estates were attacked and 15,000 plantation Tamils became refugees over-night.[44] Thirty towns in five provinces were also affected by the violence and the death toll was seventeen. The workers including women and children who were attacked ran into jungles and walked from Balangoda many miles over hazardous terrain to take refuge in Bogowantalawa. The National Council of the Ceylon Workers Congress meeting in emergency session on 29 August 1981 issued a statement condemning the violence Extracts from the statement.

"This wave of violence has left a trail of destruction and desolation, misery and suffering ..... Plantation workers have once again been forced to flee their line rooms: have been

---

[44] ibid., Page

made targets of hoodlums and thugs who have had a field day, looting, murdering, maiming and raping these defenceless people. Thousands have been rendered destitutes with nothing in the world except the tattered rags which cover them.

The attack on the plantation workers which seemed to have followed a pattern, passes understanding in the light of the fact that they, as President (Jayewardene) very succinctly summed up, were not guilty of any political offence, while on the other hand contributed to enriching the economy of this country, with their blood, sweat and tears, bones, flesh and every sinew. These acts of unbridled terrorism which for the second time in four years rendered a community of dignified hard working people refugees, forced to live on the charity of public, have also brought into sharper relief, the stark realities that they are by no means secure and safe in particular areas of the country when the passion and beastly instincts of certain people rise uppermost outweighing reason and rationale."[45]

The Ceylon Workers Congress, called upon the government to 'appoint an impartial probe to investigate and ascertain the causes of these incidents and those who were responsible for them.'

The government failed to take any measures to bring the offenders to book and murderers went scot free.

Following the 1977 and 1981 violences many plantation Tamils had sought refuge in Vavuniya where they were rehabilitated by the social service organisation, Gandhiyam. (The Gandhiyam Secretary Dr. Rajasundaram was later murdered in Welikade prison in July 1983 along with 52 other Tamil political prisoners. Gandhiyam was never allowed thereafter to revive). The Gandhiyam established settlements and housed nearly

---

[45] CWC Report of Activities 1979   1981. Page 34

40,000 plantation Tamils who had been severely affected by the 1977 and 1981 violences. Beginning from 16th November 1981 on the pretext of hunting for "terrorists" hundreds of soldiers descended on the settlements. People were assaulted and Gandhiyam officials were hung upside down and tortured. Houses were searched and women were sexually abused. The Movement for Inter-Racial Justice and Equality in a letter to President Jayawardene in January 1982 said :-

"The saddest aspect of the attacks is that the victims were hill-country Tamil plantation workers who suffered tremendously in recent racial riots and came as refugees to settle down in Vavuniya. They had begun their new life with hope, clearing the jungle, building homes and cultivating their garden plots in spite of several hardships. The soldiers and police mercilessly ran over by foot and truck, and destroyed the plantations on which these poor people depend for their livelihood. The people were pulled out from their homes in the dark, harassed and questioned till evening without breakfast and lunch. The soldiers were provided food by helicopters. After the attacks, the people looked dehumanized and mentally tortured and spoke to us with tears showing signs of fear and mental agony."

During 1982 and 1983 the attacks on Gandhiyam continued with blessings from the Government and farms, houses and crops were destroyed by soldiers. The organisers and other officials of Gandhiyam were arrested under the Prevention of Terrorism Act and held in custody.

THE 1983 GENOCIDAL MASSACRE

Beginning from 24th July 1983 the worst violence against the Tamils in the history of Sri Lanka shook the country. The reason for the violence has been attributed by politicians and the media to the killing of the thirteen soldiers in Jaffna on the night of 23rd July 1983, although organised violence against Tamils had begun in Jaffna, Vavuniya and Trincomalee in

March 1983 itself and there is ample evidence that the country wide violence had been planned and elements within the government had taken an active role in the planning and execution. T.D.S.A. Dissanayake wrote that 'there was organised violence by gangs which were quite obviously trained and who operated with military precision.'[46]

Minister of State Anandatissa de Alwis, appearing on TV on 29th July 1983 had this to say :

"......... the looters ...... carried lists of names and addresses. They knew exactly where to go...... Therefore there was pre-planning. We now understand from the information in the hands of the government that these names and addresses were taken from the Register of Electors, from the Parliamentary Voters lists, and were prepared very much in advance for an occasion such as this....."

Tamils were sought out in every village, and town and irrespective of age or sex were battered, beaten, shot or cut with swords and knives to death; many were burnt alive. Even patients in hospitals were killed. Tamil houses were burnt; shops, Hindu temples and schools were destroyed. Nearly 2,000 Tamils had been killed within two weeks and nearly 150,000 persons sought asylum in refuge camps. The police and the armed forces took active part in the violence and assisted thugs to murder and destroy. Wherever Tamils attempted to defend themselves, the police or the army rushed to the scene and dealt with the "cheeky" Tamils.

Once again the plantation areas were severely affected. Some towns in these areas were completely destroyed and entire families were wiped out. Hundreds of thugs went into estates in Badulla, Welimada, Passara, Madulsima, Hali Ela, Yattinuwara,

---

[46] 'The Agony of Sri Lanka'   T D S A Dissanayake, 1984

Bandarawela and Kandapola and killed workers, looted and burnt their line rooms.

The following statistics relating to the violence in the plantation areas were recorded by B.A. Ajantha, after a field research, although he admits that this is not an exhaustive list covering the entire plantation area."[47]

Destruction

Houses	1488
Shops	1049
Temples	5
Schools	3
Cinemas	2
Vehicles	145
Factories	10
Line Rooms	44 sets
(nearly 450 units)	

Murders	141	
Refugees (in camps)	29,682	

(However it has to be noted that many incidents not known to the writer have not been included in the above figures)

During June and July 1983 Tamil plantation refugees in Trincomalee were subject to harassment by the security forces. They were attacked and their huts were burnt. On 24th July 1983 several hundred Tamil refugees in the area were rounded up by the navy and forcibly taken in buses to Nuwara Eliya and other plantation areas where violence was raging, to be left on the sides of roads at the mercy of blood thirsty hooligans.

The Ceylon Workers Congress(CWC) which is a constituent part of the present government in a statement issued after an

---

[47] 'Sri Lanka: July 1983   Violence Against Indian Tamils'   Ajantha, TIC, Madras

emergency meeting of its National Council on 14th August 1983 said :

"We are deeply grieved that this wave of violence has been unleashed even before the wounds inflicted by the criminals in August 1981 had healed. The vast majority of peace loving Tamils, who by hard work and frugality have helped to build the economy of this country, have been rendered destitute overnight. Official statistics are an underestimate of the actual casualties and extent of damages caused."

The statement pointed out that the violence was carried out after a carefully hatched plan over a long period of time :

"Even before the riots began in Colombo, the attack on the Tamil settlers in Mannar, Vavuniya and Trincomalee areas had been set in motion. It is significant that communal violence on a large scale commenced with the burning of the Trincomalee settlers' huts. They were uprooted from their homes in the early hours of July 24th morning, bundled and brought against their will to Nuwara Eliya and Hatton and left as destitutes.

The failure of the Minister of Lands and Land Development (Gamini Dissanayake) to give shape and content to a decision of the cabinet to regularise the land holdings of stateless persons and other people of Indian origin in the North through dialogue with the Minister of Rural Industrial Development and President of the Ceylon Workers Congress (S. Thondaman), has been a major contributory factor to this sad state of affairs which we are witnessing today.

Instead of implementing the declared policy regularising the settlements of persons of Indian origin in these areas, where they were transported and dumped as refugees after the previous holocausts, a concerted attempt had been made by officials to drive them out of their holdings under various false pretexts. This had been further intensified around the middle of July when the police and security personnel set in motion a wave of terror intimidating the settlers and driving them away.

In order to legalise this programme, the Minister of Lands and Land Development has submitted a proposal 'for prevention of encroachments and illicit settlements in Sri Lanka, the prevention of unlawful activities in any individual, group of individuals, Associations, organisations or body of persons within Sri Lanka ....' which gives wide powers to the Minister and includes some of the obnoxious provisions of the Prevention of Terrorism Act, like detention without trial by order of the Minister of Lands for upto 18 months, power to Government Agent or Assistant Government Agent, without going to courts or authorise police, army or navy to demolish buildings etc. thus branding settlers as terrorists."[48]

The July 1983 genocidal massacre left deep wounds in the hearts and minds of the Tamils, including the plantation Tamils and resulted in an exodus to India and other countries.

AFTER JULY 1983

After July 1983, particularly from the beginning of 1984 the situation in the North and the East deteriorated with the security forces and home guards going on the rampage often, murdering civilians innocent of any crime, raping, looting, burning whole villages and arresting thousands of youths. Although the situation in the plantation areas was apparently calm, Tamils were being harassed to such an extent that an explosive situation was imminent. The Tamil plantation workers had to bear this harassment in addition to the economic and other burden heaped on them.

Many plantation Tamil youths were arrested under the Prevention of Terrorism Act and held in custody without access

---

[48] CWC Report of Activities 1982   1984, Page 25

to parents or lawyers or trial on the allegation that they had connection with the Northern and Eastern Tamil militants. A special investigation unit of the police was established in Kandy in 1985 to arrest suspected persons. This unit acted on information without ascertaining the veracity of such information and arrested many Tamils. On several occasions the unit arrested on complaints by persons who had a private score to settle. The plantation workers were appalled by this harassment and resorted on many occasions to strike action. But this did not deter the police continuing to intimidate workers. In addition the government established army camps in Nuwara Eliya, Talawakelle and Hatton. The army joined the police and caused havoc in the plantation areas affecting not only the workers but also the national economy. Local thugs also took the matter into their own hands and Tamil plantation workers who visit towns were attacked and robbed by these thugs. Tamil passengers in State-owned buses and trains too were not spared.

In 1986 the problem became worse and violence shook the plantation areas. On 27 January 1986 thugs attacked plantation Tamil workers in the Talawakelle town and burnt 18 shops belonging to Tamils. For the first time after independence, the plantation Tamils responded in kind. Several houses belonging to the Sinhalese were attacked. 40,000 workers staged a strike in protest. Thereafter Tamils were assaulted in buses and trains and in the streets and a member of a police party which went to attack Diagama Estate in Agrapatana was killed.

The government imposed curfew and arrested many Tamil youths. On 31st January 1986, Sinhalese thugs went into Darawela Estate in Hatton and burnt 17 line rooms and killed a youth. Similar attacks were carried out on St. Andrews Estate in Talawakelle. Tamil passengers passing through Ginigathena were pulled out of the buses and assaulted.

Tamil workers retaliated when they were attacked by thugs in Bogawantalawa on 2nd February 1986. Several shops and houses were burnt and one Sinhalese person was killed. By now more army personnel had been rushed to Talawakelle and Hatton and they shot dead a Tamil youth in Dickoya on Periyakendakelle Estate and another Tamil in Hatton. The army and police assisted by thugs continued to harass the Tamils throughout 1986.

On 24th February 1986 the army surrounded St.Coomb s Estate in Lindula and shot dead a child aged 2¹/₂ years and injured six other workers. As a result of this attack without any provocation, 10,000 workers in the area staged a strike demanding the removal of the army camp which had been established there. On 27th February 1986, a shop belonging to a Tamil was burnt and 5,000 workers in the area went on strike. While Tamil workers were being attacked from all sides, Gamini Dissanayake, the Minister of Lands stated in Parliament on 7th March 1986 that he had requested President Jayawardene to take action to remove knives and swords in the possession of the hill country Tamils. The object of the statement was two-fold. Firstly to give an impression that it was the plantation Tamils who were responsible for the violence in the hill country and secondly to take measures to remove any weapons that they may possess to defend themselves.

Attacks were carried out by thugs and the security personnel during the rest of the year on plantation Tamils on Dyarraba Estate, Welimada (14.4.86), Levallon Group, Gampola (21.4.86), Melton Estate, Talawakelle (25.5.86), Hatton town (2.6.86), Eildon Hall Estate, Lindula, Kelliewatte Estate, Bogawantalawa (23.6.86), Talawakelle town (28.6.86), Punduloya town and surrounding area (2.7.86), Salpilla Estate, Panwila (24.7.86), Kenilworth Estate, Ginigathena (10.9.86), Eskdale Estate, Ragala (21.10.86), North Meddecombra Estate, Talawakelle (7.12.86) and Lindula town (14.12.86)

Arrests of plantation Tamils were made by the army and police on Abbotsleigh Estate, Hatton (30.1.86), Bambarakelle

Estate, Lindula (16.2.86), Bogawantalawa (22.2.86), Patana (8.3.86), Hatton (12.3.86), Nuwara Eliya (30.5.86), Elidon Hall Estate, Lindula (11.6.86), Talawakelle and Hatton (14.6.86), Talawakelle (18.6.86), Elgin Estate, Talawakelle (26.8.86), Devon Estate, Talawakelle (4.9.86), Talawakelle town (17.9.86), Agrapatana town (22.9.86), and Abotsleigh Estate, Hatton (23.12.86).[49] Strikes by workers, protest by trade unions and several conferences held in which the police and trade unions participated, did not deter the security forces. Attacks on Tamils were continued without regard for human life or national economy. On 5th January 1987 the police shot dead three Tamil workers on St.Coomb's Estate in Lindula and injured 18 others. Attacks on Tamils were also carried out Wewessa Estate, Bandarawella (2.2.87) and Galaboda Estate, Nawalapitiya (6.2.87).

The deteriorating situation in the plantations prompted the Ceylon Workers Congress (CWC) which is part of the present government from 1978 with its President as Minister of Rural Industrial Development, to adopt a resolution at its 29th Convention held on 14th and 15th March 1987. The entire resolution is reproduced below to show the seriousness with which the Congress viewed the explosive situation on the plantations and which tantamounts to indictment on the government :

"This 29th Convention of the Ceylon Workers Congress marking the 46th Anniversary of the Organisation Meeting in Kandy on the 14th and 15th March, 1987 under the Chairmanship of President S. Thondaman resolves as follows :

VIEWS WITH ALARM

The indiscriminate arrest of plantation youths on suspicion, false tip-off and information which has created growing

---

[49] These attacks, arrests and violence have all been reported in the Sri Lankan newspapers

apprehension and discontent in the plantation areas, and that the Police and the Security Services have embarked on a witch hunt that can have far-reaching consequences,

CONSCIOUS

That the unwarranted arrest of youths on suspicion and their detention for long periods will have the most deleterious effects on the entirety of the plantation youth and community,

MINDFUL

That such arrests infuse a spirit of resentment and indignation in youth that can push them to the paths of violent resistence and activity,

CALLS UPON

The Law-Enforcement authorities to (a) desist from unwarranted arrests, detentions for long periods, assaults and inhuman treatment of those in custody which will undermine the confidence in them and in the Government; (b) Adopt a humane and pragmatic approach to these problems of a sensitive and delicate nature; (c) expedite investigations and release all those against whom no cases have been filed in Courts; (d) desist from using the Prevention of Terrorism Act in all cases which could be investigated and charges framed, if any, under the Penal Code or the ordinary Law of the Land; (e) review Police-public relations and refurbish the image of the police.

URGES

The Government to initiate procedures which will provide for meaningful consultation and co-operation of the organisations representatives of workers in matters involving the maintenance of peace and order in the plantation areas".[50]

---

[50] Resolution No.3 adopted by the CWC   29th Convention, March 1987

7

FUTURE OF THE PLANTATION TAMILS

The Universal Declaration of Human Rights (quoted earlier) declares that 'every one has the right to a nationality' and that 'no one shall be arbitrarily deprived of his nationality' (Article 15). These provisions were inserted in the draft Declaration in view of the large number of stateless persons in existence after the Second World War and in order that 'individuals should not be subjected to actions such as was taken during the Nazi regime when thousands had been stripped of their nationality by arbitrary government action'[51].

Richard B. Lillich commends the insertion of the article, since many rights under international and national law depend upon a person having nationality and as the first step to eradicate statelessness, thus offering all individuals access to such rights[52]. When the United Nations was taking steps to eradicate statelessness, Sri Lanka proceeded without any qualms to create statelessness arbitrarily depriving a million people of their nationality, an action comparable to the measures of the Nazi regime, in the same year of the adoption of the Universal Declaration of Human Rights. Human rights activists in the plantations have observed that thousands of Tamils will continue to be stateless for several more years, if not decades, despite the new Act 'promising' citizenship due to the extremely slow rate at which citizenship is being granted.

---

[51] Global Protection of Human Rights by Richard B. Lillich in 'Human Rights in International Law, Legal and Policy Issues' - Ed. Theodor Meron, Volume 1, Page 153

[52] ibid., page 154

Article 9 of the Convention on the Reduction of Statelessness specifically provides that 'a contracting party may not deprive any person or group of persons of their nationality on racial, ethnic, religious or political grounds'. Although Sri Lanka has not ratified this Convention for obvious reasons, the moral obligation cast on a State to conform to UN Conventions particularly those which directly and wholly affect them, cannot be denied. Canada, the Federal Republic of Germany, Norway and the United Kingdom are among the countries which have ratified the Convention and these countries which continue to grant massive aid to Sri Lanka annually, appear unconcerned by the violation of human rights of the plantation Tamils. It must be pointed out that such grant of aid without any check on human rights by these countries which 'speak' so much about human rights, has encouraged the Sri Lankan government to violate human rights with impunity.

Sri Lanka has ratified the following international human rights instruments:

1. International Covenant on Economic, Social and Cultural Rights.
2. International Convenant on Civil and Political Rights.
3. International Convention on the Elimination of All Forms of Racial Discrimination.
4. International Convention on the Suppression and Punishment of the Crime of Apartheid.
5. Convention on the Elimination of All Forms of Discrimination Against Women.
6. Convention on the Prevention and Punishment of the Crime of Genocide.
7. Slavery Convention of 1926 as amended.
8. Supplementary Convention on the Abolition of Slavery, the Slave Trade, and Institutions and Practices Similar to Slavery.
9. Convention for the Suppression of the Traffic in Persons and the Exploitation of the Prostitution of Others.
10. Convention on the Nationality of Married Women.

Sri Lanka has also made a Declaration recognising the competence of the Human Rights Committee under Article 41 of the International Covenant on Civil and Political Rights.[53] But it has not ratified the Optional Protocol to the Civil Rights Covenant. In 1982 Sri Lanka deposited a Unilateral Declaration against Torture with the United Nations.[54]

Article 2(2) of the International Covenant on Economic, Social and Cultural Rights states that the States Parties undertake to guarantee that the rights enunciated in the Covenant will be exercised without discrimination of any kind as to race, colour, sex, language, religion, political or other opinion, national or social origin, property, birth or other status. Article 2(1) of the International Covenant on Civil and Political Rights similarly states that the States Parties undertake to respect and to ensure to all individuals within its territory and subject to its jurisdiction the rights recognized in the Covenant, without distinction of any kind, such as race, colour, sex, language, religion, political or other opinion, national or social origin, property, birth or other status.

The United Nations Declaration on Elimination of All Forms of Racial Discrimination provides in Articles 1 and 2 as follows:

Article 1 - "Discrimination between human beings on the ground of race, colour or ethnic origin is an offence to human dignity and shall be condemned as a denial of the principles of the Charter of the United Nations, as a violation of human rights and fundamental freedoms proclaimed in the Universal Declaration of Human Rights, as an obstacle to friendly and peaceful relations among nations and as a fact capable of disturbing peace and security among peoples."

---

[53] 'Human Rights International Instruments: Signatures, Ratifications, Accessions etc.' UN   ST/HR/4/Rev.4, 1982

[54] 'Human Rights Violations in Sri Lanka'   Brian Senewiratne, page 1

Article 2(1) "No State, institution, group or individual shall make any discrimination whatsoever in matters of human rights and fundamental freedoms in the treatment of persons, groups of persons or institutions on the ground of race, colour or ethnic origin.

Article 2(2) No State shall encourage, advocate or lend its support, through police action or otherwise, to any discrimination based on race, colour or ethnic origin by any group, institution or individual."

The International Convention on the Elimination of All Forms of Racial Discrimination also contains similar provisions.

All these Conventions and Covenants recognize several other rights and States Parties ratifying these instruments would be expected to act in conformity with the spirit of the provisions. But Sri Lanka has shown scant regard for the provisions of international human rights instruments despite ratification. All forms of racial discrimination are practised and the plantation Tamils are particularly selected as targets as a group. The international jurist Paul Sieghart describes the plight of the plantation Tamils of Sri Lanka in the following words:

"However there is one community in Sri Lanka that has every justification for seeing itself as a grossly underprivileged minority, and that is the so-called 'Indian Tamils. The bulk of these continue to work on the tea estates, and by their labour make a vast contribution to the national income. Yet they continue to be miserably paid, miserably housed and miserably deprived in the provision of food, health and education. For none of these deprivations do they have any remedy, since most of them cannot now even be represented in Parliament or in local government; although virtually all of them today were born in Sri Lanka, the great majority do not now even have Sri Lankan citizenship.[55]"

---

[55] 'Sri Lanka: A Mounting Tragedy of Errors' Paul Sieghart, ICJ, 1984. page 13

It is not only the discriminatory acts or omissions of the governments and government institutions directed at them that affect the plantation Tamils. Discriminatory measures against Tamils in general, such as in relation to employment, education and use of language, religion etc. also have the effect of making their life miserable. The Official Language Act of 1956 made Sinhala as the official language of Sri Lanka in terms of which Tamil public servants were required to obtain proficiency in the Sinhala language. The 1972 and 1978 constitutions gave constitutional status to the Sinhala Language, as the official language. The effect of the Official Language Act and the several Treasury Circulars and Public Administration Circulars (not less than 25 circulars have been issued) on employment to Tamils in public service is described in a study entitled 'State Sector Employment and Tamils in Sri Lanka' by a Group of Researchers:

"During this quarter century period, a good number of old-entrants have either retired prematurely or retired on reaching the age of optional retirement i.e. 55 years. The intake of Tamils to the various categories of Public servants have virtually minimised if not dried up ..... The bivalent prime motive of Sinhala as the one Official Language in (1) eschewing out the Tamils from the public services and (2) serving as a bottle neck with regard to Tamils entering into the Public Service have been achieved, and is safely entrenched."[56]

Relatively, few plantation Tamils entered public service as a result of discrimination in education and recruitment policy and even those who entered were affected by the Official Language Act and the Circulars.

Although the Sri Lanka constitution provides that a person is entitled to receive communications from, and to communicate

---

[56] 'State Sector Employment and Tamils in Sri Lanka' - Theepam Institute, 1987, page 72

with any official in his official capacity (Article 22 (1) (a)) in Tamil, letters from government institutions to Tamils are sent in the Sinhala Language, sometimes with translation in English. This is practiced even today despite protests by Tamil parties and organisations. This attitude of government officials has created extreme difficulty for the plantation Tamils, many of whom do not understand either of the languages.

Article 24 (1) of the Constitution further provides that the language of the Courts throughout Sri Lanka will be Sinhala, with a proviso that the language of courts exercising original jurisdiction in the Northern and Eastern provinces will be Tamil. Majority of the plantation Tamils live in the Central, Sabaragamuwa and Uva provinces and their language (Tamil) may not be used in the courts in these provinces and consequently most plantation Tamils appearing in courts in these provinces would not understand the proceedings.

From what has been said thus far, it would be obvious to readers that the plantation Tamils are a very oppressed minority in Sri Lanka and perhaps in the world. They are discriminated in every sphere of life and it is tragic that successive governments, which are elected to protect people, have played leading roles in the oppression of the plantation Tamils. All discriminatory measures are entrenched in the Constitution, Laws and regulations and even an impartial government in the future would take years, if not decades, to dismantle the discriminatory shell that has been constructed. The recent history of Sri Lanka is replete with incidents of politicians resorting to discrimination for narrow political self interests. Therefore it would be futile to expect that such an impartial government would be established in the foreseeable future. In addition plantation Tamils have been repeatedly subject to genocidal massacres, grievous injury, rape and torture and their property has been plundered and destroyed. Scores of youths in the plantation have been arrested and held in custody, tortured and some have been sentenced to long periods of imprisonment under the obnoxious Prevention of Terrorism Act.[57]

From past experience and present trends it may be reasonably concluded that discrimination and violence against the plantation Tamils would continue endlessly and that they should seek ways and means to extricate themselves from the clutches of oppression.

MIGRATION TO NORTH AND EAST

Many people who are interested in the problem of the plantation Tamils have suggested that they should migrate to the North and East where Tamils are a majority community and some have even stated that the entire plantation Tamil population should be moved to the North and East under a government programme. After 1970 Sri Lankan and plantation Tamil communities realised that discrimination against Tamils would continue if there was no solidarity among the two communities and preventive measures were not taken. The most powerful union in the plantations, the Ceylon Workers' Congress (CWC), which has a political wing recognised by the Elections Commissioner as a political Party, joined the Tamil Congress (TC) and the Federal Party (FP) in 1972 to form the Tamil United Front (TUF). However in 1976 when the TUF reconstituted itself to form the Tamil United Liberation Front (TULF) with the avowed aim of reconstituting the Tamil Nation-State which had been amalgamated with the rest of the island by the British in 1833, the CWC chose not to participate in the TULF, because of the opinion that such reconstitution, though a possible solution to the problems of the Tamils in the North and East, would not be a solution to the Tamils in the plantations and that separation of the North and East would trigger a massacre of the plantation Tamils. But genocidal massacres began to occur from 1977 even without separation.

---

[57] In the beginning of 1987 a Tamil-speaking youth was sentenced to 20 years rigorous imprisonment under the PTA for alleged concealment of information - The Exodus, Vol.2 No.6, February 1987

After the 1977 and 1981 genocidal massacres large numbers of plantation Tamils to move to the North and East, it must be observed that this movement is as a result of compulsion caused by violence. They would not have moved from the hill country, if they were allowed to live in peace and conditions were created for peaceful coexistence with the Sinhalese. But it is important to note that despite the violence, the vast majority of the Tamils have not moved from the plantations.

Plantation Tamils have lived in the hill country areas (see Map 1 in Appendix) for nearly 150 years and there cannot be any doubt as to their right to continue to live there. One has to remember that sovereign States have been established by migratory populations in the last two centuries. Even large nations like the United States of America and Australia were created by migratory populations, while indigenous populations in these countries have been relegated to obscurity.

THE RIGHT OF SELF DETERMINATION

Whatever the course of action that is to be followed, it is essential that the right of self determination of the plantation Tamils is recognised. At the Thimpu (Bhutan) Conference between the Tamils and Sri Lankan government, the Tamil representatives placed 'recognition of self determination of the Tamil people' as one of their four demands. The government delegation rejected this demand along with the other demands. The International Covenants on Civil and Political Rights and the Economic, Social and Cultural Rights to which Sri Lanka is a signatory recognize that 'all peoples have the right of self determination', and that 'by virtue of that right they freely determine their political status and freely pursue their economic, social and cultural development'. It has been stated by jurists that a legal right to self determination arises insofar as parties to the covenants are concerned although there is controversy over the definition of the 'people'.[58]

---

[58] Political and Related Rights by John P. Humphrey in 'Human Rights in International Law: Legal and Policy Issues' Ed. Theodor Meron, Volume 1, page 195

The plantation Tamils are a national minority and a national minority has been defined as 'a group in a country which possesses, and has a common will — however conditioned to preserve certain habits and patterns of life and behaviour which may be ethnic, cultural, linguistic, or religious, or a combination of them and which characterize it as a group'.[59]

As in the case of the Tamils of the North and East, the plantation Tamils constitute an ethnic group with a separate language and have preserved their culture, religions, patterns of life and behaviour, against tremendous odds ranging from discriminatory legislation to violence amounting to genocide. In this context it may be mentioned that the plantation Tamils have always been treated and recognized as a separate people. Governments have nominated Members of Parliament to represent the plantation Tamils when there were no elected representatives. In the all-important Bandaranaike-Chelvanayakam Agreement (26 July 1957) a distinct reference was made in regard to the plantation Tamils.[60]

"Regarding the question of Ceylon citizenship for people of Indian descent and revision of the Citizenship Act, the representatives of the Federal Party put forward their views to the Prime Minister and pressed for an early settlement.

The Prime Minister indicated that this problem would receive early attention."

At the Thimpu Conference which began on 12th August 1985 the government delegation questioned the right of the Tamil representatives to represent or negotiate on behalf of

---

[59] 'The International Protection of Minorities'   Professor James Fawcett, Minority Rights Group, Report No.41, 1979, page 4

[60] The Bandaranaike   Chelvanayakam Agreement entered into on 26 July 1957 between S J V Chelvanayakam on behalf of the Tamils and the then Prime Minister S W R D Bandaranaike, which envisaged certain measure of autonomy for the Tamils was unilaterally abrogated later by the Government.

the plantation Tamils, thereby taking up the position that the plantation Tamils are a separate people with separate problems. Delimitation Commissions have considered the plantation Tamils separately and in the Census Reports they have been enumerated separately since 1911. The Donoughmore and the Soulbury Commissions made separate recommendations for these Tamils and number of other Commissions and Committees such as the Jackson Committee (1938) and the Majoribanks and Marakkayor Committee (1917) have been appointed to study the special problems of the plantation Tamils. Many laws and regulations, including those which are discriminatory, have been made specifically for these Tamils. Most important of all, the plantation Tamils feel that they are a distinct people and they have preserved and endeavour to protect their culture, religion, language, territory and their way of life and a consciousness of brotherhood pervades the entire community.

It must also be noted that they have been in occupation of definable territory in the island. In the Nuwara Eliya district the Tamils form 60.8% of the population, of whom 47.3% are Plantation Tamils and together with the Tamil-speaking Muslims form 63.6%. If Kandy, Badulla and Nuwara Eliya districts are taken together the Tamils form 28.4% of the population of whom 21.3% are plantation Tamils and the Tamil-speaking population in these three districts is 35.1%. If all the plantation districts are taken together, i.e. (Kandy, Nuwara Eliya, Matale, Badulla, Kegalle, Kalutara, Ratnapura and Monaragala districts) Tamils form 18.2% of the population of whom 13.6% are plantation Tamils and the Tamil-speaking population forms 23.1%. Although the Tamils are a minority in each of these districts except the Nuwara Eliya district, it is possible to carve out a contiguous area within these districts which would have a Tamil majority. Creation of such a new district for the Tamils, appears to be the only way to ensure that plantation Tamils are adequately represented, protected from violence and continue to exist as a group of people in a country where discrimination and violence are rife and continuous attempts are being made to dismember the group. Carving out·separate districts and electorates are not new to Sri Lanka. The Seruwila electorate and the Digamadulla (Amparai) electoral district were carved out so that such district or electorate would have a Sinhalese majority in Tamil majority areas. Therefore precedence exists for the carving out of an area for the plantation Tamils. If such an area is carved out it is possible, if the people so decide, for the area to have institutional links with the North and East for the promotion of matters such as language, culture and education (See Map 2 in Appendix for suggested area).

INTERNATIONALISATION

An important aspect that has to be considered by the representative organisations is the internationalisation of the issue of the plantation Tamils. The film by Granada on British Television titled 'Is This Your Cup of Tea' in 1974 drew wide attention and brought about pressure on the then employer-companies and the Sri Lankan government. Such measures are frequently necessary, so that the international community is made aware of the truth through the world media. This would not be too difficult for the trade unions. The plantations trade unions are affiliated directly or indirectly to international trade union bodies such as the International Confederation of Free Trade Unions (ICFTU), World Federation of Trade Unions (WFTU) and the International Federation for Plantation, Agricultural and Allied Workers (IFPAAW). These bodies have tremendous influence in the international scene and the plantation trade unions have only to decide to request these international bodies for support in the campaign. It would be worthwhile to remember that a greater tragedy relating to the ethnic problem in Sri Lanka was averted primarily due to the internationalisation of the problem.

THE QUESTION OF GENOCIDE

The question must surely be asked, what is the ultimate objective of all these discriminations over several years culminating in terrible violence against the Tamils in Sri Lanka. In this context it is appropriate to quote a passage from the book 'Axis Rule in Occupied Europe' by Raphael Lemkin:

"Generally speaking, genocide does not necessarily mean the immediate destruction of a nation, except when accomplished by mass killings of all members of a nation. It is intended rather to signify a coordinated plan of different actions aiming at the destruction of essential foundations of the life of national groups, with the aim of annihilating the groups themselves. The objectives of such a plan would be the disintegration of political and social institutions, of culture, language, national feeling, religion, and the economic existence of national groups, and the destruction of personal security, health, dignity, and even the lives of the individuals belonging to such groups. Genocide is directed against the national group as an entity, and the actions involved and directed against individuals, not in their individual capacity, but as members of the national group'.[61]

The Convention on the Prevention and Punishment of the Crime of Genocide defines genocide in the following words:

"In the present Convention, genocide means any of the following acts committed with intent to destroy, in whole or in part, a national, ethnical, racial or religious group, as such:

a) Killing members of the group;
b) Causing serious bodily or mental harm to members of the group;
c) Deliberately inflicting conditions of life calculated to bring about its physical destruction in whole or in part;
d) Imposing measures intended to prevent births within the group;
e) Forcibly transferring children of the group to another group.

---

[61] Quoted by Leo Kuper in 'Prevention of Genocide', page 9

The International Convention on the Suppression and Punishment of the Crime of Apartheid, while including similar provisions as the Genocide Convention, in defining 'apartheid' also states that apartheid would include 'any legislative measures and other measures calculated to prevent a racial group or groups from participation in the political, social, economic and cultural life of the country and the deliberate creation of conditions preventing the full development of such a group or groups, in particular denying to members of a racial group or groups basic human rights and freedoms.'

There could be no doubt from these definitions in the conventions that apartheid is commonly practised in Sri Lanka and the process of genocide goes on.

The statements of leading politicians in the government party, the Opposition and other leading citizens in the country and the actions such as torture, rape, burning of whole villages, mass murders, enactment of legislation to make easy crimes such as murder, large scale bombings of Tamil civilian areas and condonement of crimes and numerous other acts, leave no room for doubt that genocide is definitely in the minds of those who planned and perpetrated these gruesome acts and given the opportunity would not hesitate to continue to commit and complete the crime of genocide. It is also pertinent to mention here that during the July 1983 genocidal massacre, to cause loss of life and damage to property in such gigantic proportions at least a million people would have participated directly or indirectly in the destruction.

The methods of the Nazi rule are relevent in this context. A foremost authority on genocide, Professor Leo Kuper writes about the prelude to genocide by the Nazis:

"The Nazis had systematically prepared the ground for the destruction of human rights, and ultimately for genocide, by statutory enactment, judicial process, and bureaucratic regulation, thus substituting tyrannical and murderous Rule By Law for the Rule of Law".[62]

It has to be pointed out at this stage that no mention is made in the Indo-Sri Lanka Accord of 1987 (29 July 1987) about the plantation Tamils, except repatriation of those Tamils already granted Indian citizenship and the Tamil refugees in India (Clause 2.16 D). It is surprising that such an important accord should exclude the plantation Tamil population who have been victims of violence and suffer the same insecure position of the Tamils of the North and East. It would appear that they have been excluded from the Accord to give the impression that they do not suffer any disability and face no danger.

The following two statements made by the President of the country himself and the Minister of Lands indicate the extreme danger that can befall the plantation Tamils and the Sri Lankan Tamils living in the South:

"If the government of India wants to invade they can take over Sri Lanka in less than 24 hours and arrest me. But if that happens then all the Tamils living among the Sinhalese will be finished."-
President Jayewardene.[63]

"They are bringing an army from India. It will take 14 hours to come from India. In 14 minutes, the blood of every Tamil in the country can be sacrificed to the land, by us"-
Gamini Dissanayake
Minister of Lands at the meeting of the LJEWU at the UNP head-quarters in Colombo on 5th September 1983.[64]

---

[62] 'Prevention of Genocide'   Leo Kuper, 1984, page 30

[63] India Today   15.12.85.

[64] 'Sri Lanka: Racism and the Authoritarian State'   Race & Class, Vol.XXVI No.1, 1984, Race Relations Institute, London, page 81

In this climate it is necessary to take preventive measures so that a catastrophe would be avoided. The international community has an important role to play in the events in Sri Lanka, particularly those relating to the plantation Tamils. In the event of the failure of the international community in the dismantling of all discrimination and an end to all violence, the plantation Tamils would be left with no other alternative than the final action, as warned in the Preamble to the Universal Declaration of Human Rights:

"Whereas it is essential, if man is not to be compelled to have recourse, as a last resort, to rebellion against tyranny and oppression that human rights should be protected by the Rule of Law."

It is hoped that the plantation Tamil community of Sri Lanka is not left by itself to be destroyed like so many minority groups because of lack of international concern, and care by the family of the United Nations. The plantation Tamil awaits his destiny. The veteran plantation trade unionist (late) C.V. Velupillai lamented thus:[65]

> What man dare speak
> His fettered, unbroken
> Days of drudgery...
> That sole legacy
> From sire to son!
> Harried by debt
> Poverty and shame
> Bound to the cart-wheel
> A beast of burden
> Cowed and bent
> To a lesser beast
> An outcast,
> From the mainland
> And here a helot
> Stripped of his name
> A reproach and danger
> To his kin and clime
> He bides his time
> For a destiny.

[65] 'In Ceylon's Tea Garden'   C V Velupillai, 1980

MAP 1

SRI LANKA

PLANTATION TAMILS

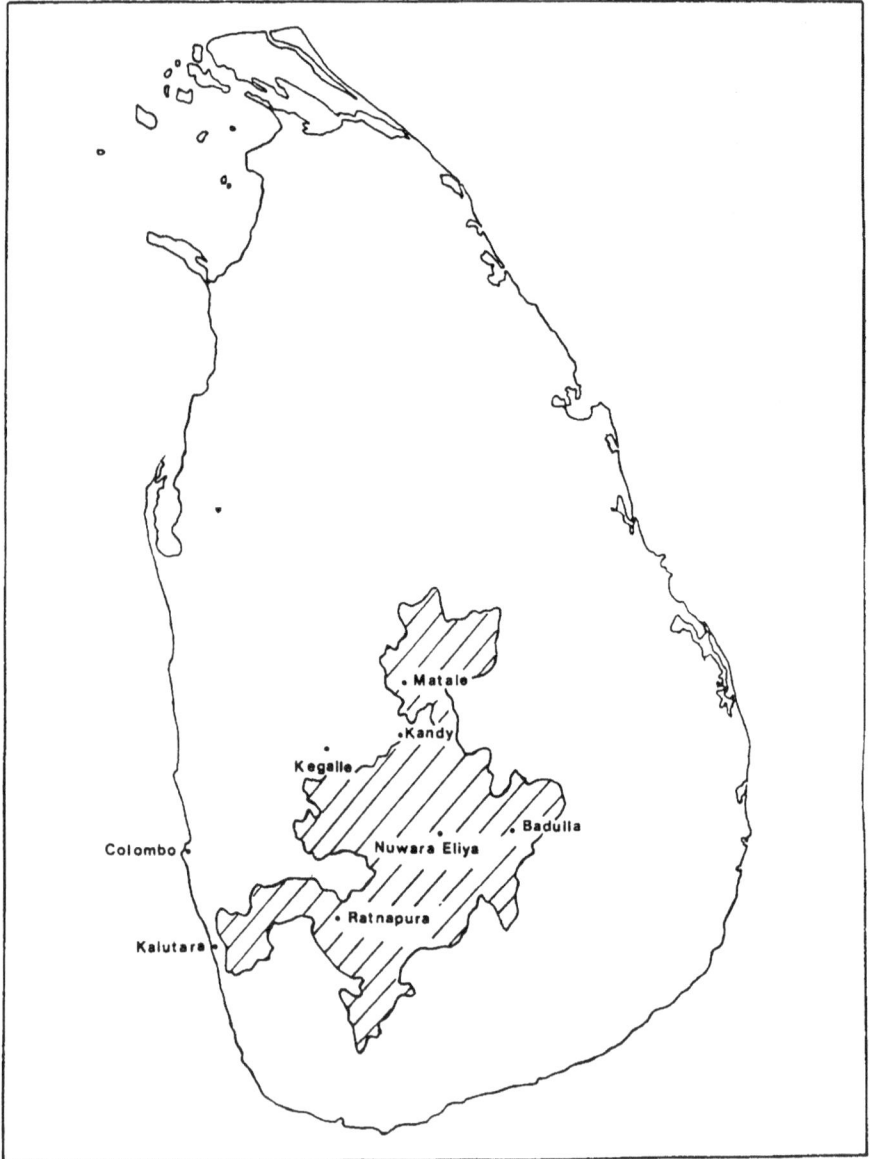

MAP 2

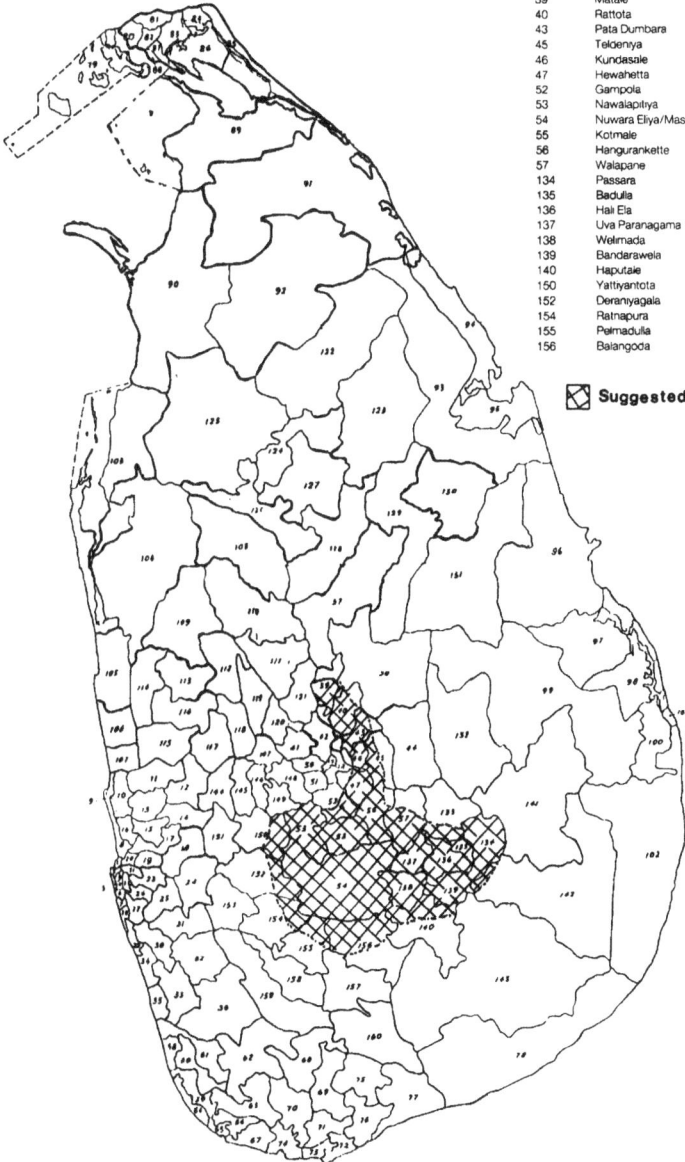

Suggested Plantation Tamil District

ELECTORAL DISTRICTS

Electoral Number	Districts
39	Matale
40	Rattota
43	Pata Dumbara
45	Teldeniya
46	Kundasale
47	Hewaheta
52	Gampola
53	Nawalapitiya
54	Nuwara Eliya/Maskeliya
55	Kotmale
56	Hangurankette
57	Walapane
134	Passara
135	Badulla
136	Hali Ela
137	Uva Paranagama
138	Welimada
139	Bandarawela
140	Haputale
150	Yatiyantota
152	Deraniyagala
154	Ratnapura
155	Pelmadulla
156	Balangoda

⬧ Suggested Area

MAP 3

INDIA AND SRI LANKA

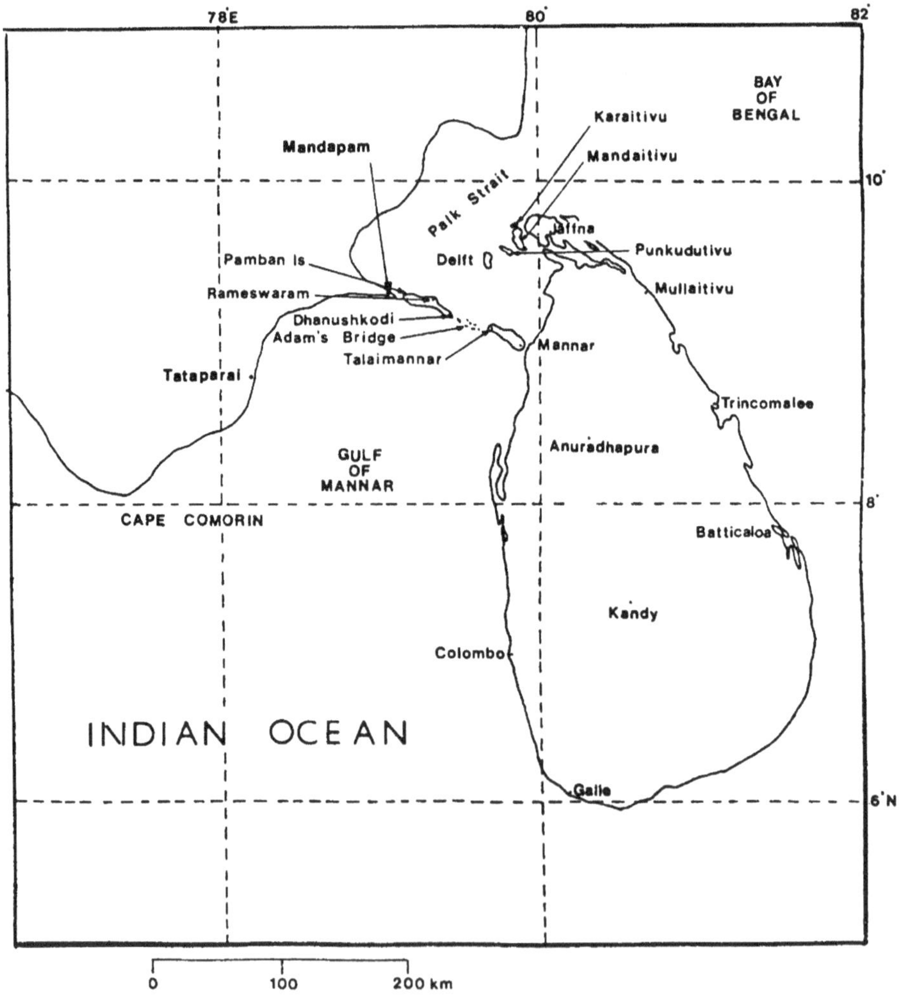

78°E
80°
82°
10°
8°
6°N
BAY OF BENGAL
Karaitivu
Mandaitivu
Mandapam
Palk Strait
Jaffna
Punkudutivu
Delft
Pamban Is
Mullaitivu
Rameswaram
Dhanushkodi
Adam's Bridge
Talaimannar
Mannar
Tataparai
Trincomalee
Anuradhapura
GULF OF MANNAR
CAPE COMORIN
Batticaloa
Kandy
Colombo
INDIAN OCEAN
Galle
0
100
200 km

MAP 4

SRI LANKA
PROVINCES

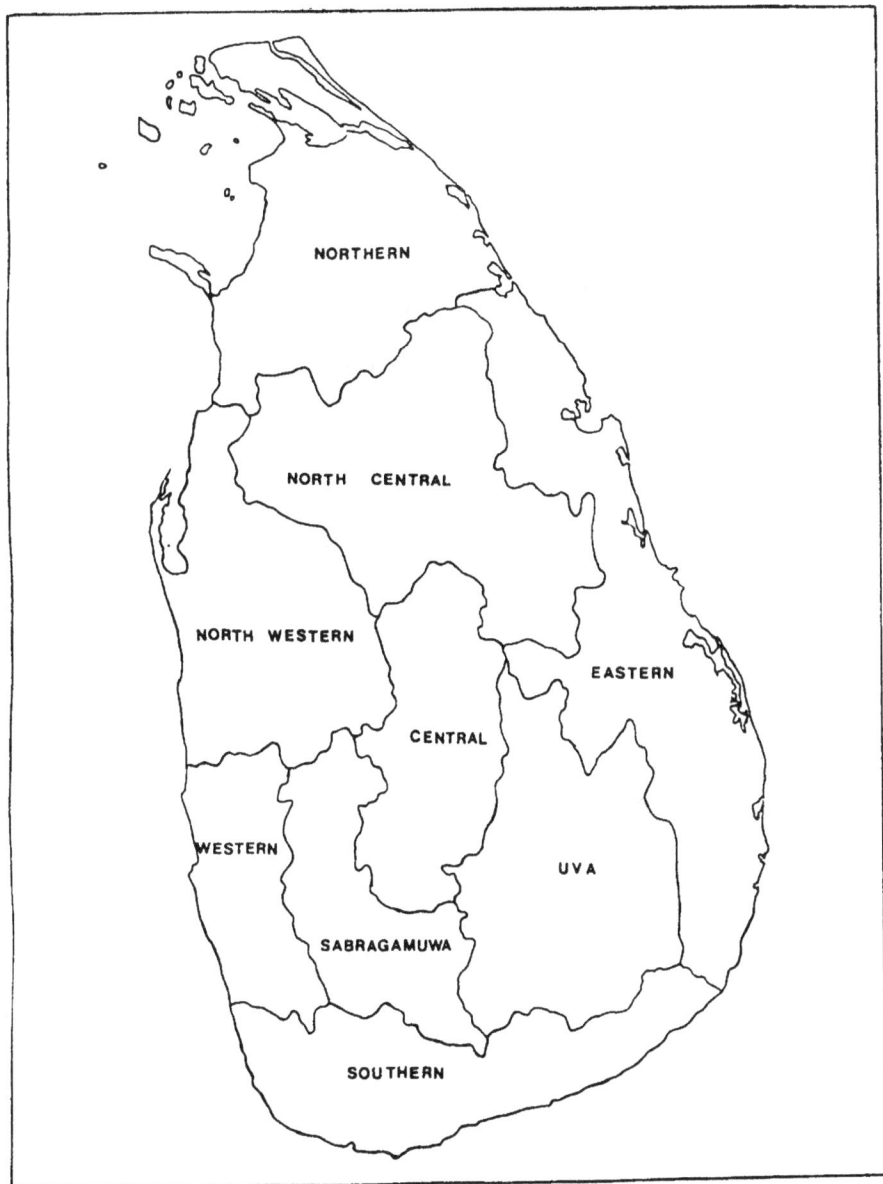

NORTHERN

NORTH CENTRAL

NORTH WESTERN

EASTERN

CENTRAL

WESTERN

UVA

SABRAGAMUWA

SOUTHERN

0   50   100 km

MAP 5

SRI LANKA

DISTRICTS

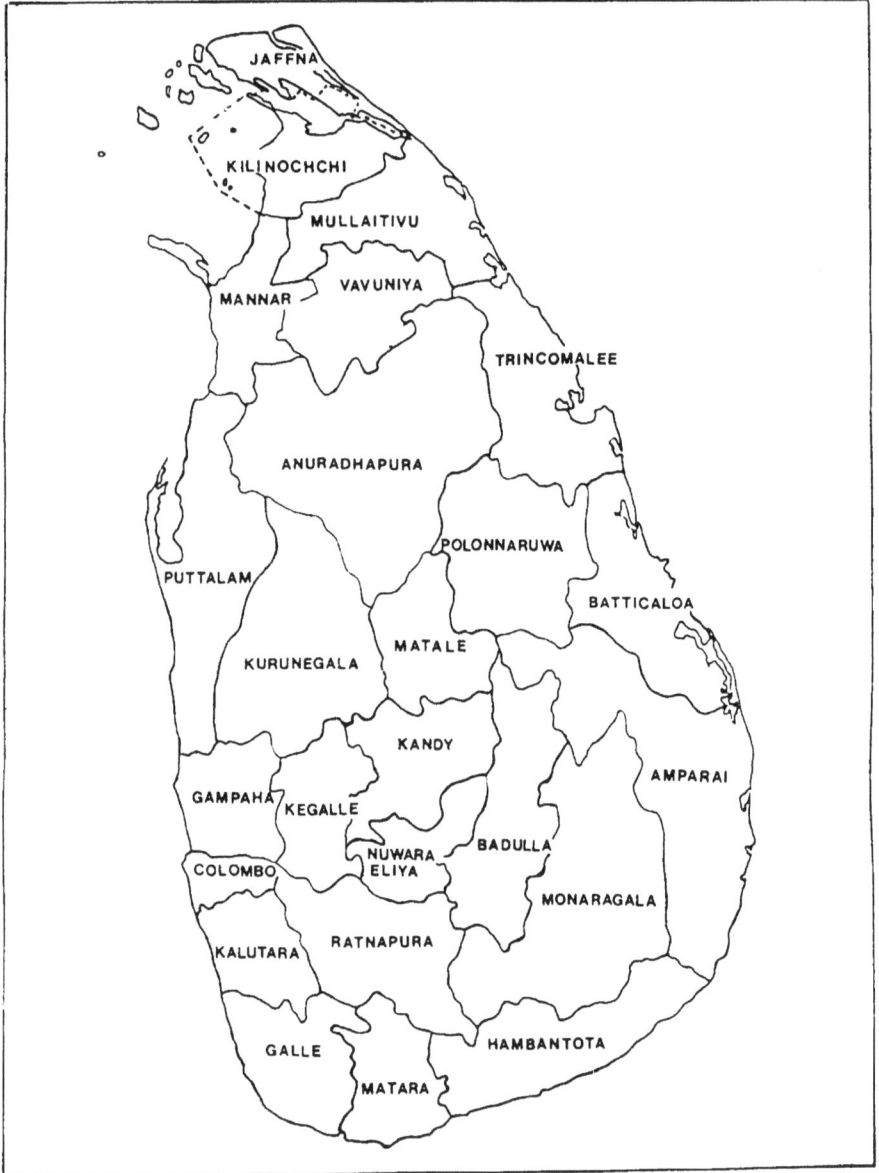

JAFFNA

KILINOCHCHI

MULLAITIVU

VAVUNIYA

MANNAR

TRINCOMALEE

ANURADHAPURA

POLONNARUWA

PUTTALAM

BATTICALOA

MATALE

KURUNEGALA

KANDY

AMPARAI

GAMPAHA

KEGALLE

NUWARA
ELIYA

BADULLA

COLOMBO

MONARAGALA

KALUTARA

RATNAPURA

GALLE

HAMBANTOTA

MATARA

0   50   100 km

APPENDIX

TABLE XIII

POPULATION OF PERSONS OF INDIAN ORIGIN 1911 - 1981

Year	Total Sri Lankan Population	Total Persons of Indian origin		Indian origin on Plantations		
		Indian Origin Absolute No.	%	Absolute No. Indian Origin	As a % of Population	
1911	4,106,350	530,983	12.9	457,765	86.2	
1921	4,497,854	602,510	13.4*	493,944	82.0	
1946	6,657,339	780,589	11.7	665,853	88.8	
1953	8,097,895	974,098	12.0	814,000	83.6	
1963	10,590,060	1,122,850	10.6	932,090	82.5	
1971	12,711,143	1,174,606	9.2	951,785	81.9	
1981	14,850,001	825,233	5.6	N/A	N/A	

SOURCE: DEPARTMENT OF CENSUS & STATISTICS, SRI LANKA

N/A – Not available

98

TABLE XIV

REPRESENTATION IN PARLIAMENT 1947 TO 1977

	Total	Sinhalese	Sri Lankan Tamils	Tamils of Indian Origin	Muslims
Population 1946	1008	69.48	11.08	11.78	7.08
Seats due on basis of population	95	66	12	10	6
Seats Obtained					
1947	95	68	13	7	6
1952	95	75	13	Nil	6
1956	95	75	12	Nil	7
Population 1958 (Estimate)	1008	69.38	10.98	12.08	6.38
Seats due on basis	151	106	17	18	10
Seats Obtained					
March 1960	151	123	18	Nil	9
July 1960	151	122	18	Nil	11
1965	151	121	17	Nil	11
1970	151	123	19	Nil	8
Population 1971	1008	71.98	11.18	9.48	7.08
Seats due on basis of Population	168	121	19	16	12
Seats Obtained					
1977	168	136	19	1	12

Source: Reports of the Delimitation Commissions and 'Electoral Politics in an Emergent State' by A. Jeyaratnam Wilson

TABLE XV

CRUDE DEATH RATES ACCORDING TO ETHNIC GROUPS
1971 - 1976

Ethnic Group	1971 No. of Deaths	1971 Death Rate	1972 No. of Deaths	1972 Death Rate	1973 No. of Deaths	1973 Death Rate	1974 No. of Deaths	1974 Death Rate	1975 No. of Deaths	1975 Death Rate	1976 No. of Deaths	1976 Death Rate
Sinhalese	62,229	6.9	66,328	7.2	66,422	7.1	74,611	7.8	76,983	7.8	71,153	7.1
Sri Lanka Tamils	11,693	8.3	12,135	8.4	11,463	7.8	12,217	8.2	11,712	7.6	11,543	7.4
Indian Tamils	15,679	13.4	17,309	14.5	14,915	12.3	24,106	19.6	17,317	16.0	15,859	14.8
Sri Lanka Moors	6,527	7.9	7,042	8.4	6,819	8.0	7,378	8.5	7,761	8.5	6,959	7.5
Burghers and Eurasians	460	10.2	448	9.7	437	9.3	412	8.6	422	9.0	386	8.3
Malays	244	5.7	227	5.2	237	5.3	288	6.4	274	6.0	234	5.0
Indian Moors	110	4.1	124	4.4	102	3.6	132	4.6	111	4.0	149	5.1
All Ethnic Groups	97,209	7.7	103,918	9.1	100,678	7.7	119,518	9.0	115,101	8.5	106,506	7.9

SOURCE: Sri Lanka : Report of Mission on Needs Assessment for Population Assistance - UNFPA - 1980

SELECT BIBLIOGRAPHY

Arumugam V, *Discrimination in Education* (Theepam Institute, Jaffna, 1982)

Bond, Edith M, *The State of Tea* (War on Want, March 1974)

Chattopadhyaya H P, *Indians in Sri Lanka* (OPS Publishers, Calcutta, 1979)

Ceylon Repatriates Association, *Aliented Everywhere* (Tamil) (Kodaikkanal, Tamil Nadu, 1984)

Ceylon Workers Congress, *Plantations Strike 1984* (Colombo, 1984)

De Silva K M, *A History of Sri Lanka* (Hurst, London, 1981)

Federal Party, *Memorandum on the Constitution Submitted to the Constituent Assembly* (Colombo 1972)

Gnanamuttu G A, *Education and the Indian Plantation Worker in Sri Lanka* (Colombo 1977)

Hillier, Stella and Lynn Gerlach, *Whose Paradise   The Plantation Tamils of Sri Lanka* (Minority Rights Group, London, May 1987)

Jayawardena, Kumari, *Ethnic and Class Conflicts in Sri Lanka* (Centre for Social Analysis, Dehiwela, Sri Lanka, 1985)

Jayawickrama, Nihal, *Human Rights: A Sri Lankan Experience 1947-1981* (PhD Thesis, University of London, 1983)

Kuper, Leo, *International Action Against Genocide* (Minority Rights Group, London, 1982)

------------ *The Prevention of Genocide* (Yale University Press, 1985)

Kurian, Rachel, *The Position of Women Workers in the Plantation Sector in Sri Lanka* (ILO, 1981)

Manor, James, Ed. *Sri Lanka in Change and Crisis* (Croom Helm, London, 1984)

Meron, Theodor, Ed. *Human Rights in International Law: Legal and Policy Issues*, Volumes I & II (Oxford University Press, 1984)

Mohanaraj, *Neo-Slavery in the Twentieth Century* (History of the Up-Country Tamils (Tamil) (Eelam Research Organisation, United Kingdom, 1984)

Navaratne P, *Wages, Terms and Conditions of Employment in Sri Lanka* (Friedrich Ebert Stiftung, Colombo, 1983)

Peries L L T, *The Citizenship Law of the Republic of Sri Lanka* (Government Printers, Sri Lanka, 1974)

Ponnambalam, Satchi, *Sri Lanka: National Conflict and the Tamil Liberation Struggle* (Tamil Information Centre & Zed Books, London, 1983)

Rote, Ron, *A Taste of Bitterness - The Political Economy of Tea Plantations in Sri Lanka* (Free University Press, Amsterdam, 1986)

Sajhau, Jean-Paul & Jurgen Von Muralt, *Plantations and Plantation Workers* (ILO, 1987)

Sieghart, Paul, *Sri Lanka: A Mounting Tragedy of Errors* (International Commission of Jurists, March 1984)

---------- *The International Law of Human Rights* (Oxford University Press, 1983)

Senewiratne, Brian, *Human Rights Violations in Sri Lanka* (Melbourne, 1985)

Singh, I J Bahadur Ed. *Indians in South Asia* (Sterling Publishers, New Delhi, 1984)

Tamil Information Centre, *Sri Lanka: July 1983 Violence Against "Indian Tamils"* (Madras, 1983)

Tamil Rescue Appeal, *Genocide of Tamils and Human Rights Violations in Sri Lanka* (London, 1984)

Tamil United Liberation Front, *Memorandum of Discrimination Submitted to the International Commission of Jurists* (Colombo, 4th September 1973)

Theepam Institute, *State Sector Employment and Tamils in Sri Lanka* (Jaffna, January 1987)

Velupillai C V, *Born to Labour* (M D Gunasena, Colombo, 1970)

ABBREVIATIONS

CEEF	*Ceylon Estates Employers Federation*
CIC	*Ceylon Indian Congress*
Col	*Cost of Living*
CWC	*Ceylon Workers Congress*
DWC	*Democratic Workers Congress*
FP	*Federal Party*
GCE	*General Certificate of Education*
ICFTU	*International Confederation of Trade Unions*
IFPAAW	*International Federation of Plantation Agricultural and Allied Workers*
ILO	*International Labour Organisation*
IYSH	*International Year of Shelter for the Homeless*
JEDB	*Janatha Estates Development Board*
LJEWU	*Lanka Jathika Estates Workers Union*
MP	*Member for Parliament*
NLR	*New Law Reports*
NUW	*National Union of Workers*
SLFP	*Sri Lanka Freedom Party*
SLSPC	*Sri Lanka State Plantations Corporation*
TC	*Tamil Congress*
TUF	*Tamil United Front*
TULF	*Tamil United Liberation Front*
UN	*United Nations*
UNICEF	*United Nations International Childrens Emergency Fund*
UNP	*United National Party*
WFTU	*World Federation of Trade Unions*
WHO	*World Health Organisation*

INDEX

www.ingramcontent.com/pod-product-compliance
Lightning Source LLC
Chambersburg PA
CBHW050533280326
41933CB00011B/1569